Trendsetting Essays On AI And Law

Advanced Series On
Artificial Intelligence (AI)
And Law

Dr. Lance B. Eliot, MBA, PhD

ISBN: 978-1-95-738601-0

DEDICATION

To my incredible daughter, Lauren, and my incredible son, Michael.

Forest fortuna adiuvat (from the Latin; good fortune favors the brave).

CONTENTS

Note: Visuals are collected together in Appendix B, rather than being interjected into the chapter contents, for ease of reading, enhanced flow, and to see the visuals altogether.

ACKNOWLEDGMENTS

I have been the beneficiary of advice and counsel by many friends, colleagues, family, investors, and many others. I want to thank everyone that has aided me throughout my career. I write from the heart and the head, having experienced first-hand what it means to have others around you that support you during the good times and the tough times.

To renowned scholar and colleague, Dr. Warren Bennis, I offer my deepest thanks and appreciation, especially for his calm and insightful wisdom and support.

To billionaire and university trustee, Mark Stevens and his generous efforts toward funding and supporting the Stevens Center for Innovation.

To Peter Drucker, William Wang, Aaron Levie, Peter Kim, Jon Kraft, Cindy Crawford, Jenny Ming, Steve Milligan, Chis Underwood, Frank Gehry, Buzz Aldrin, Steve Forbes, Bill Thompson, Dave Dillon, Alan Fuerstman, Larry Ellison, Jim Sinegal, John Sperling, Mark Stevenson, Anand Nallathambi, Thomas Barrack, Jr., and many other innovators and leaders that I have met and gained mightily from doing so.

Thanks to Ed Trainor, Kevin Anderson, James Hickey, Wendell Jones, Ken Harris, DuWayne Peterson, Mike Brown, Jim Thornton, Abhi Beniwal, Al Biland, John Nomura, Eliot Weinman, John Desmond, and many others for their unwavering support during my career.

Thanks goes to the Stanford University CodeX Center for Legal Informatics and the Stanford University Computer Science department for their generous support, and for the insightfual and inspirational discussions and feedback from my many fellow colleagues there.

And most of all thanks as always to Lauren and Michael, for their ongoing support and for having seen me writing and heard much of this material during the many months involved in writing it. To their patience and willingness to listen.

CHAPTER 1
INTRODUCTION TO AI AND LAW

This book provides a series of crucial essays encompassing the burgeoning field of AI and the law.

These essays are ostensibly standalone and do not require any prior familiarity with the AI and law topic. You are welcome to read the essays in whichever order you might prefer. The essays have been numbered and sequenced as chapters for ease of referring to the discussions and not due to any need to read one before another.

The essays provide a helpful overview and entry point into the field of AI and law. You will find the essays relatively easy to read and eschew arcane techno-terminology, aiming to layout the vital aspects in clear language and seeking to be readily grasped. The chosen topics entail the latest and hottest trends in the AI and law arena.

For those of you that are potentially interested in knowing more about AI and the law in a deeper way, you might consider my two other books on this subject:

- *"AI and Legal Reasoning Essentials"* by Dr. Lance Eliot
- *"Artificial Intelligence and LegalTech Essentials"* by Dr. Lance Eliot

Those are more akin to textbook-style orientations to the AI and the law field. Both books are available on Amazon and at major bookseller sites. The first book listed provides a comprehensive and detailed exploration of AI and law, while the second book tends to focus primarily on LegalTech and the blending of AI.

One of the most frequent questions that I get asked during my webinars, seminars, and college courses about AI and the law consists of what the phrase "AI and the law" actually refers to.

That's a fair question and deserves a useful answer. In a moment, I will borrow from my other books to provide an explanation about the meaning of "AI and the law" and then dovetail into a brief indication about each of the essays contained in this collection.

Per the essays, you'll end up seeing that there is a great deal of enthusiastic spirit for AI and the law, and likewise a sizable dollop of angst and trepidation about the intertwining of the two. In my view, whether you love it or hate it, there is no stopping the steamroller moving ahead that is going to infuse AI together with the law.

I would urge that any lawyer worth their salt ought to be learning about AI and the law. This will assuredly be especially important for those that are just now starting their legal careers, which I mention because the odds are that the convergence of AI and the law will have an especially pronounced effect throughout your lifelong legal efforts.

For those of you that might be going a more so academic route in the legal realm, rather than being a practitioner of the law per se, the beauty of AI and the law is that there is ample room for new research and a grand opportunity to make a demonstrative mark on the field.

Despite the fact that the field of AI and the law has been studied for many years, dating back to the beginning of the AI field itself, please be aware that we have only scratched the surface on this interweaving. Anyone with a desire to push the boundaries of these two realms will readily find plenty of rampways to do so.

If you are curious about the possible research avenues to pursue, make sure to take a look at my book on *AI and Legal Reasoning Essentials* since it provides a solid foundation on the research to-date and postulates what might be coming down the pike in future research activities. I bid you welcome to the field and wish you the best of luck in your endeavors.

AI And Law

In my viewpoint, Artificial Intelligence (AI) and the field of law are synergistic partners. The intertwining of AI and Law can generally be categorized into two major approaches:

- **AI as applied to Law**
- **Law as applied to AI**

Let us consider each of those two approaches.

AI As Applied To Law

AI as applied to law consists of trying to utilize AI technologies and AI techniques for the embodiment of law, potentially being able to perform legal tasks and undertake legal reasoning associated with the practice of law. Those scholars, experts, and practitioners that have this focus are using AI to aid or integrate artificial intelligence into how humans practice law, either augmenting lawyers and other legal professionals or possibly replacing them in the performance of various legal tasks.

Crafting such AI is especially hard to accomplish, problematic in many ways, and there have been and continue to emerge a myriad of attempts to achieve this difficult goal or aspiration. The rise of LegalTech and LawTech, which is modern digital technology used to support and enable lawyers, law offices, and the like throughout the practice of law are gradually and inexorably being bolstered by the addition of AI capabilities.

There are many indications already of this trend rapidly expanding in the existing and growing LegalTech and LawTech marketplace. Notably, the potent AI and LegalTech/LawTech combination has been drawing the rapt attention of Venture Capitalists (VCs). According to figures by the National Venture Capital Association (NVCA), the last several years have witnessed VC's making key investments of over one billion dollars towards law-related tech startups, many of which have some form of an AI capability involved.

Most of the AI developed so far for LegalTech and LawTech is only able to assist lawyers and legal professions in rather modest and simplistic ways. For example, AI might speed-up the search for documents during e-discovery or might enhance the preparation of a contract by identifying pertinent contractual language from a corpus of prior contracts.

Where the field of applying AI to law is seeking to head involves having AI that can perform legal minded tasks that human lawyers and other legal professionals perform. In essence, creating AI systems that can undertake legal reasoning. This is commonly referred to as AI for Legal Reasoning (AILR).

In a sense, legal reasoning goes to the core of performing legal tasks and is considered the ultimate pinnacle as it were for the efforts to try and apply AI to law. It is undoubtedly one of the most exciting areas of the AI-applied-to-law arena and one that holds both tremendous promise and perhaps some angst and possible somber qualms.

Law As Applied To AI

The other major approach that combines AI and law focuses on the law as applied AI. This is an equally crucial perspective on the AI and law topic.

Sometimes this is also referred to as the **Governance of AI**, though there are those that believe that to be a somewhat narrower perspective on the topic. In any case, the focus is primarily on the governance of AI and how our laws might need to be revised, updated, or revamped in light of AI systems.

You likely already know that AI is experiencing quite a resurgence and has become a key focus of the tech field, along with gaining attention throughout society. AI is being rapidly infused into a wide variety of industries and domain specialties, including AI in the financial sector, AI in the medical domain, and so on.

This rapid pace of AI adoption has opened the eyes of society about the benefits of AI but also has gradually brought to the forefront many of the costs or negative aspects that AI can bring forth. Some assert that our existing laws are insufficient to cope with the advances that AI is producing.

Thus, the need to closely examine our existing laws and possibly revamp them for an era and future of ubiquitous AI.

Expected Impacts

Let's consider how AI and the law can impact those in the AI field, and also contemplate how it can impact those in the field of law.

If you are an AI specialist, you should certainly be interested in the AI and law topic, either due to the possibilities of advancing AI by discovering how to leverage AI into the legal domain or due to the potential of how existing and future laws are going to impact the exploration and fielding of AI systems.

If you are a lawyer or legal specialist, you ought to be interested in the AI and law topic too, for the same reasons as the AI specialist, though perhaps with some added stake in the game.

What is the added stake?

If AI can ultimately become advanced enough to practice law, there is concern by some that it could potentially replace the need for human lawyers and other human legal-related law practitioners.

Some liken this to the famous and telling remark about commitment as exhibited via a chicken and a pig. A chicken and a pig are walking along and discussing what they might do together, and the chicken offers that perhaps they ought to open a restaurant that serves ham-n-eggs. Upon a moment of reflection, the pig speaks up and says that if they did so, the chicken would only be involved (making the eggs), while the pig would end-up being fully committed (being the bacon).

In that sense, AI specialists in this topic are involved, while legal specialists and lawyers are committed.

Meanwhile, for those of you squarely in the field of law, lest you think that AI specialists are to be spared the same fate of being overtaken by AI, you will be perhaps surprised to know that there are efforts underway to craft AI that makes AI, such as in the field of Machine Learning (ML), a specialty known as AutoML, which could potentially put human developers of AI out of a job.

What is good for the goose is good for the gander. Or, it might be that what is bad for the goose is equally bad for the gander.

About These Essays

Now that you've gotten an initial synopsis regarding the topic of AI and law, let's take a moment to briefly take a look at the essays assembled for this decisive collection.

Chapter 1 – Introduction To AI And Law

Key briefing points about this chapter:

- This book is a collection of crucial essays about AI and the law
- The essays are provided as numbered chapters (the sequence is not essential)
- AI and the law consist of two key facets
- One facet is AI as applied to the law (a mainstay of this collection)
- The other facet is applying the law to AI (i.e., governance of AI)

Chapter 2 - AI & Law: Duty To Inform

Key briefing points about this chapter:

- Attorneys have existing duties to inform and communicate with their clients
- This is generally pertinent to what is considered material matters
- Recent hubbub is that AI ought to be included in that rubric
- A new rule would be clients must be informed about any AI use by an attorney
- The same applies to any AI usage within the law practice of said attorney

Chapter 3 - AI & Law: Experimental Jurisprudence

Key briefing points about this chapter:

- A hot new trend in the law involves experimental jurisprudence or XJur
- Few everyday lawyers have heard about it, nor was it likely covered in law school
- The focus is somewhat askew of the wording since it entails studying laypersons
- And it specifically entails studying the meaning of legal concepts (it is not mock juries)
- AI is going to further enhance and bolster the emergence of experiment jurisprudence

Chapter 4 - AI & Law: Turtles All The Way

Key briefing points about this chapter:

- A legendary and somewhat unusual expression is that it is "turtles all the way down"
- This is a reference to the notion of an infinite regress and is based likely on a fable
- Supreme Court Justice Scalia famously used the expression in a SCOTUS opinion
- The expression is arising in the AI and LegalTech realm, dubiously so
- You can use the expression appropriately or use it for intentionally muddled purposes

Chapter 5 - AI & Law: Animal Rights For AI

Key briefing points about this chapter:

- There is an ongoing debate about whether AI ought to have legal rights
- Some say this is wholly premature since there isn't any sentient AI as yet
- Others believe we ought to get a handle on this now and not wait
- Rather than focusing on the applicability of human rights, another avenue is animal rights
- Animal legal rights are unsettled, boding for added confusion when being reapplied to AI

Chapter 6 - AI & Law: Language Translation Access

Key briefing points about this chapter:

- In the United States, the English language is the default language for our courts and our laws
- Having one predominant language as an underpinning provides significant benefits
- Meanwhile, those that are non-English speaking are at an inherent disadvantage
- Courts variously make use of human interpreters, though this is costly, spotty, etc.
- AI-based language translation for the spoken and written word can be leveraged by our courts

Chapter 7 - AI & Law: Legal Proximate Cause

Key briefing points about this chapter:

- The legal element of proximate cause is well-established in our courts and jurisprudence
- A key facet entails the identification of a cause or series of causes leading to an injury
- Some in AI are claiming that Machine Learning might defy proximate cause
- Few buy into that claim, a different claim about multitudes of AI systems is given more merit
- A now-classic legal research paper posits that Distributed AI (DAI) might be problematic

Chapter 8 - AI & Law: Judicial Analytics

Key briefing points about this chapter:

- Statistics can be vital to bolstering a legal argument or undercutting an opposing side
- You likely are aware that statistics can be conveniently manipulated at times
- The realm of judicial analytics leverages statistics and is a burgeoning area
- Advanced AI capabilities such as Machine Learning are being applied to judicial analytics
- Savvy lawyers need to be up-to-speed about the use of AI-boosted judicial analytics

Chapter 9 – AI & Law: Judge Breakfast

Key briefing points about this chapter:

- You would normally hope and assume that your legal arguments are the crux of your case
- The judge will dispassionately and without bias make a judicially balanced decision
- A famous line that belies this assumption is that the breakfast dining choice is crucial
- What a judge had for breakfast is a long-enduring commentary about adjudication
- The joke is worth exploring and revisiting in light of advances of AI in the judicial process

Chapter 10 - AI & Law: Lower Bound Complexity

Key briefing points about this chapter:

- Lower bound is a vital aspect of computational complexity
- When devising or comparing algorithms, the lower bound provides a key barometer
- The goal is to find the least number of steps or time required to solve a given problem
- Lawyers are somewhat faced with a similar setting when solving a legal case
- AI systems for legal reasoning will also be measured by the lower bound principles

Chapter 11 - AI & Law: Judges Gambler Fallacy

Key briefing points about this chapter:

- A simple flipping of a coin brings up some key insights about human judgment
- For a truly balanced coin, we know that there are even chances of heads or tails
- If a series of flips showcases a clump of heads or tails, we get concerned
- Turns out that court judges fall into the same trap, known as the gambler's fallacy
- AI is being used to spot these failings, though do not assume that AI cures them

Chapter 12 - AI & Law: Legal Reconnaissance

Key briefing points about this chapter:

- Discretion is a vital aspect of the law and has longstanding historical roots
- There is a dual-edged sword associated with discretion
- Trying to spot discriminatory patterns amongst discretion is logistically prohibitive
- AI can be used as a tool in ferreting out discriminatory discretion
- Efforts to pilot an AI capability coined as the Recon Toolkit are underway

Chapter 13 – AI & Law: Legal Fiction To Punish AI

Key briefing points about this chapter:

- Courts use the mechanism of legal fiction to help smooth out rough spots in the law
- A legal fiction is an assumption or acceptance of something as fact, though it might not be
- Some are proposing that AI ought to be covered via a newly conceived legal fiction
- In brief, AI would get a form of legal personhood but only in the legal fiction semblance
- This has generated intense debate and continues to be bandied about

Chapter 14 – AI & Law: Dropping The Legal Boom On AI

Key briefing points about this chapter:

- There is the famous saying that the punishment ought to fit the crime
- Ongoing debates agonize over what kind of punishment is appropriate
- Suppose that AI goes off the rails and commits crimes
- Some believe that we would need to dole out punishment to AI
- But if AI is not sentient thus this raises mindful questions about doing so

Chapter 15 - AI & Law: Not All AI Is Equal

Key briefing points about this chapter:

- Human rights are generally considered inalienable and sacrosanct
- There seems to be a tussle about human rights that we already daily contend with
- Meanwhile, some argue that AI or robots are going to need human rights
- One key issue that seems neglected is the aspect that all humans are created equal
- The same blanket statement cannot be made about AI (i.e., AI systems are unequal)

Chapter 16 – AI & Law: Legal Argumentation Uncertainty

Key briefing points about this chapter:

- Lawyers are known for their ability to craft and carryon legal arguments
- There have been efforts toward using computers for carrying out argumentation too
- AI computational argumentation continues to make progress in this realm
- The real world of arguing often includes incomplete arguments and uncertainty
- Latest advances in AI computational argumentation are adding those crucial elements

Chapter 17 - AI & Law: Winograd Scheme Challenge

Key briefing points about this chapter:

- Words matter, especially in the field of law
- A recent case was appealed due to the meaning differences of "typically" versus "normally"
- Some see daylight between those two words, others assert they are synonyms
- AI systems that use natural language capabilities are faced with similar issues
- The Winograd Schema Challenge in the AI field showcases these difficulties

Chapter 18 - AI & Law: Legal Volition

Key briefing points about this chapter:

- Volition is considered the legal core grounding of willful acts
- Mens rea sits atop volition and serves as an instantiation of a guilty mind
- We generally accept those precepts regarding humans and agency
- The question being battled is whether AI is in the same bailiwick
- Some far off futuristic AI might be, but not the AI of today

Chapter 19 - AI & Law: Shadow Docket

Key briefing points about this chapter:

- The U.S. Supreme Court has increasingly been producing so-called shadow decisions
- These are legal cases that were placed onto a shadow docket of SCOTUS
- Angst arises that the shadow case rulings are terse and without any judicial explanation
- This is said to be done for sake of expediency, though some say this is being outstretched
- AI-based legal reasoning systems are expected to be fast, so will they be shadowy too?

Chapter 20 - AI & Law: Legal Reductio

Key briefing points about this chapter:

- One of the strongest tools a lawyer can exploit entails reductio ad absurdum
- Attacking an opponent's legal posture via reductio ad absurdum can be a big win
- You have to be careful and make sure that it holds up under scrutiny
- Plus ensure that your own legal arguments aren't susceptible either
- AI legal reasoning systems are gradually coming to your aid in this regard

Chapter 21 - AI & Law: Non-Contradictions Resolute

Key briefing points about this chapter:

- Lawyers are trained to ferret out legal contradictions
- Viewed another way, the assumption is that things are to be non-contradictory
- We all seem to be abide by the law of non-contradictions
- There are lots of nuances in the line between contradictions and non-contradictions
- AI legal reasoning systems are being developed to help in these matters

Chapter 22 – AI & Law: Slipper Legal Slopes

Key briefing points about this chapter:

- We all talk about slippery slopes and routinely invoke this powerful metaphor
- This is especially true when discussing our laws and regulations
- Lawyers are apt to deal with alleged slippery slopes in the daily practice of law
- Slippery slopes are a dual-edged sword
- AI legal reasoning systems enter into the slippery slope conundrum too

Chapter 23 - AI & Law: Unintended Consequences

Key briefing points about this chapter:

- We are seemingly all used to the possibility of unintended consequences
- Some conflate unintended with unanticipated, which is no longer in vogue
- There are intended versus unintended consequences of both good and bad
- Besides unintended consequences in the law, the same can be said of AI in the law
- A four-square indication of consequences about AI and the law is depicted

Chapter 24 - AI & Law: Creative Legal Thinking

Key briefing points about this chapter:

- Being considered a creative lawyer has both merits and drawbacks
- Part of the issue is that the word "creative" invokes a wide range of connotations
- Some fervently believe that the best lawyers are in fact creative lawyers
- How can lawyers all-told can be boosted in their creativity if they wish to do so?
- AI legal reasoning systems might be one handy tool for that creativity push

Chapter 25 - AI & Law: Thinking Outside The Legal Box

Key briefing points about this article:

- People often find themselves mentally trapped inside a box, as it were
- Lawyers fall for this human foible too
- To clarify, sometimes its ok, while in other instances it is a drawback
- AI can be used as a tool to help lawyers think outside the box
- Efforts are underway to develop AI-based legal reasoning that can augment lawyers

More About This Book

For anyone opting to use this book in a class or course that pertains to these topics, note that Appendix A contains suggestions about how to use the book in a classroom setting.

Furthermore, Appendix B contains a set of slides that depict many of the salient points made throughout the book.

In some of my prior books, I've interspersed the slides into the chapter contents, but feedback by readers has generally been that readers prefer to not have the textual flow become disrupted by the slides, and instead prefer to have the supplemental material assembled altogether into an appendix.

To make sure that you are aware of those added materials, you'll notice that the ending of each chapter provides a quick reminder about the visual depictions that are available in Appendix B.

And so, with this overall orientation to the nature and structure of this book in mind, please proceed to read the essays and learn about the field of AI and law. I'm truly hoping that you'll find the essays mentally engaging and stimulative to the nature of how the law is being practiced and what the future of the law might become.

Note: *For supplemental materials depicting the aspects discussed in this chapter, refer to Appendix B, which contains various augmented diagrams, charts, and additional related facets of relevance.*

CHAPTER 2

AI & LAW: DUTY TO INFORM

Key briefing points about this essay:

- Attorneys have existing duties to inform and communicate with their clients
- This is generally pertinent to what is considered material matters
- Recent hubbub is that AI ought to be included in that rubric
- A new rule would be clients must be informed about any AI use by an attorney
- The same applies to any AI usage within the law practice of said attorney

Introduction

You've got to have nerves of steel when proposing any new rules that attorneys will need to abide by.

Any such commandments had better be ready for some quite rigorous pushback and altogether in-depth oppositional argumentation. After all, lawyers are especially adept at the art and science of making copious arguments.

You can readily bet that anytime a new rule is fostered upon attorneys and their vaunted efforts to practice law, it had better be completely thought through and have all its ducks aligned.

Indeed, there is a ruckus rapidly emerging over a potential new rule entailing a legally potent mixture that intertwines the role of attorneys, artificial intelligence (AI), and the distinguished practice of law. It is a startling brew that some lawyers find not only distasteful but imminently untenable and nonsensical.

Let's take a brief look at the ostensibly offending notion.

A recently released report by The Law Society of England and Wales has created a stir due to an indication that suggests attorneys ought to have a compelling duty to inform their clients whenever the said attorney or their law office is making use of AI in its legal efforts (the July 2021 report is entitled "Law Society LawTech and Ethics Principles" and authored by Stephanie Boyce).

Furthermore, if that doesn't get your angst going, the notification of informing the client is supposed to also include having your client provide a signed informed consent specifically pertaining to the AI usage aspects. This might be a bridge too far, namely that it is one matter to tell a client that AI is being used and perhaps a disturbingly heightened hurdle of requiring a client to sign off on it. Clients already are bombarded with various signings and adding one more could be the last straw on the camel's back.

Some retort that this is not a big deal and merely is just another inconspicuous straw needle in a large haystack of paperwork that clients are supposed to be informed about. Ergo, adding something about an AI-related usage notification is not of any notable consequence. Just plop the bureaucratic gobbledygook in front of the client when they sign-up and be done with all this crocodile tears outcry, they say.

Existing Views About AI And Law Practices

Attorneys that are savvy about AI are quick to point out that the ABA has already proffered official advice about the topic of AI usage and the practice of law. According to the ABA resolution adopted in August 2019, here's the deal about AI: "RESOLVED, That the American Bar Association urges courts and lawyers to address the emerging ethical and legal issues related to the usage of artificial intelligence ("AI") in the practice of law including (1) bias, explainability, and transparency of automated decisions made by AI; (2) ethical and beneficial usage of AI; and (3) controls and oversight of AI and the vendors that provide AI."

But wait for a second, you might exhort, there is nothing in that narrative that stipulates a rule about informing clients regarding AI usage of an attorney or law practice, and nor any stated requirement to garner signed informed consent from the client.

Okay, fair enough, so we can consider other avenues of advisory remarks that might be applicable.

In an ABA posting of August 26, 2019, entitled "Artificial Intelligence and the Law: The ABA's Important and Timely Contribution" and written by Nicolas Economou, there is this relevant narrative: "In addition to the other duties already identified, lawyers have an explicit duty to communicate to their clients material matters in connection with the lawyers' services. This duty is set out in ABA Model Rule 1.4. Other jurisdictions have adopted similar rules. Thus, not only must lawyers be competent in the use of AI, but they will need to understand its use sufficiently to explain the question of the selection, use, and supervision of AI tools."

Not wanting to split hairs, but there isn't anything in there either that categorically requires a particular duty associated with a rather strict nature of informing a client and getting informed consent. A seemingly reasonable interpretation is that attorneys need to be competent in the use of AI (when applicable to their efforts), for which, they should also aim to achieve a level of understanding that they can sufficiently explain the AI usage to their clients.

That is a vast difference.

How do some make that stretch and land on the must-tell about AI supposition?

You can try to stridently tie the AI topic to the notion that lawyers have a duty to communicate to their clients on material matters underlying the lawyers' services. Thus, logically, if AI is, in fact, being used such that it is within the rubric of seemingly material matters, you could claim that silently and subtly this implies that an attorney does have a duty to directly, explicitly, and presumably with confirmation included, ensure that they communicate about AI to a client.

This gets fuzzy very quickly.

Imagine that a lawyer is using an ordinary online search engine that just so happens to have an AI component embedded in the search feature. Does this usage come within the strictness of informing a client and getting informed consent about AI usage?

Ridiculous, some would assert.

Let's try another example. A contract management software package is being used in a law office. It has a natural language processing (NLP) capability. This allows for the attorneys and legal professionals to bring up contract passages via entering relatively fluent English sentences rather than resorting to the use of narrowly specified commands. Though this is getting perhaps closer to the crux of things in terms of AI-related material use, it still seems to fall short.

Some would argue that the idea of adding a rule about AI usage would be pertinent once we have bona fide AI legal reasoning systems. Until then, this effort to highlight and overly inflate the importance of AI in today's legal efforts is sorely misguided and outrightly unwarranted.

Conclusion

You be the judge, should you set aside any qualms about this for now or should you seek to get ahead of the game and ensure you are fully capable of informing your clients about AI usage at your law practice?

That's a judgment you'll need to make, for now.

.

Note: *For supplemental materials depicting the aspects discussed in this chapter, refer to Appendix B, which contains various augmented diagrams, charts, and additional related facets of relevance*

CHAPTER 3
AI & LAW: EXPERIMENTAL JURISPRUDENCE

Key briefing points about this essay:

- A hot new trend in the law involves experimental jurisprudence or XJur
- Few everyday lawyers have heard about it, nor was it likely covered in law school
- The focus is somewhat askew of the wording since it entails studying laypersons
- And it specifically entails studying the meaning of legal concepts (it is not mock juries)
- AI is going to further enhance and bolster the emergence of experiment jurisprudence

Introduction

Experimental jurisprudence.

It is up and coming. Some would say it is an especially hot topic and the latest and greatest thing since sliced bread.

I dare say that most day-to-day lawyers have likely not heard of experimental jurisprudence. Indeed, you might be surprised to know that it isn't even what you likely assume or think it is.

How so?

Per the consensus of numerous researchers and legal scholars, experimental jurisprudence entails performing empirical studies that focus on non-lawyers. Furthermore, the crux of the undertaking involves ascertaining how non-lawyers or so-called *legally unfamiliar laypersons* interpret or have some overall understanding of legal concepts.

That is probably a lot narrower of a designation than the typical attorney might otherwise assume from the combination of those two words, namely the denoting of this legal domain as consisting of experimental jurisprudence. You would seemingly see the word "experimental" and be under the distinct impression that empirical efforts are included, which is indeed the case (you are on the mark so far). You would next see the word "jurisprudence" and undoubtedly be under the impression that this has to do with the law and perhaps adjudication of one kind or another (you are kind of right).

What you might not immediately have gathered from the moniker is that it is purposefully limited in its inquiry by two key respects: (1) that the human subjects or participants being studied are solely laypersons and not lawyers and thus tends to exclude anyone that has substantive expertise in the law, (2) the element of inquiry is about human cognition and narrowly so in the specific niche regarding beliefs about legal concepts.

So, in that sense, you might have initially and mistakenly thought about studies involving jurors and how they deliberate during court cases as being squarely in the realm of empirical jurisprudence. You would generally be wrong or at least askew of what empirical jurisprudence is currently intended to be about. This is decidedly not the same as those mock jury or mock judging experiments, though there is likely to be overlapping elements worthy of mindful due consideration.

Grasping The Significance Of Experimental Jurisprudence

Perhaps an exemplar would be helpful to articulate the fine line involved.

Consider the concept labeled as *reasonableness.*

The law frequently refers to reasonableness as a crucial component of jurisprudence. A probing question during a court case might be whether someone acted reasonably. Was there a semblance of reasonableness about what took place? As you know, there is a tremendous amount of latitude encompassing that which is reasonable versus that which is unreasonable. This is a potentially thorny, nebulous, or certainly highly malleable concept that can vary demonstratively from case to case.

An experimental jurisprudence approach would seek to empirically try to ascertain what reasonableness means to laypeople.

This might be dramatically different than the meaning usually ascribed by lawyers and judges. By doing an analysis of non-lawyers and making those results known, specialists that practice the law and lawmakers that make the laws are presumably going to be more informed about what those vital concepts signify to those not versed in the law.

You see, lawyers and those immersed in the law are at times in an echo chamber or a bubble, completely preoccupied with what those in the legal profession have to say. Empirical jurisprudence can provide a glimpse beyond the bubble and offer valuable insights accordingly. The typical kinds of legal concepts being analyzed include aspects entailing the conceptual meaning of reasonableness, property, punishment, causation, consent, intent, recklessness, and so on.

A handy and quite detailed overview of experimental jurisprudence will be published next year in the *University of Chicago Law Review* and has conveniently been posted as a preprint entitled "Experimental Jurisprudence" (authored by Kevin Tobia of the Georgetown University Law Center).

This excellent paper examines several ongoing myths about what experimental jurisprudence consists of. A noteworthy historical aspect mentioned in the paper is that even though the modern-day definition of experimental jurisprudence was first established in 2014 in a *Harvard Law Review* article, the initial origins trace back some fifty years ago (but, at that time embodied a markedly different meaning which has been wholly rebooted).

If you want to impress your colleagues that you are an insider when it comes to knowing about experimental jurisprudence, you can casually mention that you are knowledgeable about XJur. Yes, the use of *XJur* is a catchy acronym that legal specialists are using when collegially referring to this budding field of expanding interest.

Per Tobias, there are two central questions for Xjur to address: "(i) What is the relationship between ordinary and legal concepts? (e.g., is the legal concept of causation different from the ordinary one?), (ii) What are the criteria of legal concepts? (e.g., what is the appropriate criterion for deciding when something is a legal cause?)".

I'll give you another important reason to care about experimental jurisprudence. It is a topic that is going mainstream and you don't want to be left behind, especially as someone steeped in the law. In the July 23, 2021 issue of *Science*, an article by Roseanna Sommers introduces experimental jurisprudence to non-lawyer scientists, technologists, and engineers that might wish to contribute to the burgeoning realm. This does make sense since as pointed out in the ostensibly widely circulated piece: "Looking to the future, experimental jurisprudence scholars are expected to use a growing set of methodologies: neuroimaging, computational and corpus linguistics, cross-cultural studies, and developmental work with participants across the age spectrum."

In my particular line of work, consisting of AI and the law, the use of artificial intelligence (AI) is equally contributory to experimental jurisprudence. AI can substantively be used to aid in modeling the conceptual underpinnings of legal concepts. Advanced techniques incorporating knowledge maps and machine learning can readily be useful tools in this arena.

Conclusion

Now that you have a taste of what experimental jurisprudence entails, you are in the know and on your way to utilizing Xjur if the time comes.

That being said, some assert that experimental jurisprudence is a fad and it will eventually dissipate and lose its appeal. Perhaps it will be once again rebooted anew further down the road. On the other hand, here's what the *Science* article boldly postulates: "As experimental jurisprudence gains traction, it may someday come to be an influential methodology that informs legal scholarship and practice, taking its place alongside economics, history, sociology, critical theory, and philosophy."

If so, I'd like to politely and humbly remind you that you first heard about it here.

Note: *For supplemental materials depicting the aspects discussed in this chapter, refer to Appendix B, which contains various augmented diagrams, charts, and additional related facets of relevance.*

CHAPTER 4

AI & LAW: TURTLES ALL THE WAY

Key briefing points about this essay:

- A legendary and somewhat unusual expression is that it is "turtles all the way down"
- This is a reference to the notion of an infinite regress and is based likely on a fable
- Supreme Court Justice Scalia famously used the expression in a SCOTUS opinion
- The expression is arising in the AI and LegalTech realm, dubiously so
- You can use the expression appropriately or use it for intentionally muddled purposes

Introduction

Attorneys love to make use of clever sayings or catchy expressions. The law is ostensibly about words and their meanings, thus there is an intrinsic fascination by lawyers about how we say things and what we intend to convey.

I'd like to cover one expression that might be unfamiliar to you, or you might vaguely know but have rarely ever used or seen used. I'm referring to the vaunted notion that it might be *turtles all the way down.*

If you've not come across those sage words, you might be a bit bewildered by what it portends.

Let's take a look.

There are numerous claims of how the expression came to be. The usual backstory is that it came from the earliest efforts to figure out what the earth is composed of. The standard answer at the time was that the earth is made of rocks.

When you pointedly inquired about what is underneath the rocks, the brisk reply was that there are rocks under the rocks. Daring to ask again, you might further inquire what's underneath the rocks that are underneath the rocks, which the person answering might shrug their shoulders and make a tiresome sigh, and then indicate it is rocks all the way down.

Okay, that explains about rocks, but this abundantly seems to skirt the aspect about the turtles. How did we go from rocks to having turtles in this picture?

A variant of the rocks-oriented tale is that there is a long-standing mythological story about what keeps the world seemingly from falling endlessly as though it is unsupported from below. Some believed that the planet was simply a gigantic ball that ought to be dropping eternally into the forever abyss of outer space. To this, the esteemed response was that the globe is sitting on the back of a mighty turtle. What is underneath that almighty turtle? The answer is of course that there is yet another turtle acting as support of its brethren. There are (assuredly) turtles all the way down, however far you want to go.

You can handily use this expression whenever you want to describe a situation or circumstance entailing infinite regress.

Those that particularly delight in a bit of snobbishness will at times employ the turtles all the way down refrain. It could be that the elicitation of comparing something to an infinite regress is entirely on-target and appropriate, while in other instances the catchphrase is utilized as a veiled attempt to sidestep providing an actual answer.

I suppose in today's terminology, it is almost like a Jedi using their mind control to tell others that there is nothing to see here and they should move along (that's a *Star Wars* reference, for those of you that have been living under a rock or in a deep cave).

I earlier indicated you might have come across the turtle's expression while in law school. This is certainly quite possible as it was used by Supreme Court Justice Scalia in a notable SCOTUS case. The otherwise itsy-bitsy footnote that included the turtle's expression had forever landed the *turtles all the way down* into the lore of the legal jurisprudence.

The Supreme Court case of Rapanos v. United States (547 U.S. 715, 2006) dealt with the Clean Water Act and ostensibly the definition of wetlands. In short, the defendants had been accused of filling in wetlands, doing so in violation of the Clean Water Act. They appealed the case on the basis that the area being filled-in was not in fact a wetlands area. The crux of the matter came down to whether wetlands that have no discernibly potent connection to other navigable waters are within the scope of the Clean Water Act.

A plurality of the justices essentially argued that wetlands that are disconnected from navigable waters are not within the scope of the Clean Water Act. The written opinion was led by Justice Scalia, in conjunction with fellow jurists John Roberts, Clarence Thomas, Samuel Alito.

In the written opinion, they took to task the position of Justice Kennedy for a claimed somewhat farfetched or overstretched attempt at defining the scope of wetlands, including presumably distorting a prior Supreme Court ruling known as SWANCC (Solid Waste Agency of Northern Cook County v. Army Corps of Engineers): "Thus, Justice Kennedy misreads SWANCC's "significant nexus" statement as mischaracterizing Riverside Bayview to adopt a case-by-case test of ecological significance; and then transfers that standard to a context that Riverside Bayview expressly declined to address (namely, wetlands nearby non-navigable tributaries); while all the time conceding that this standard does not apply in the context that Riverside Bayview did address (wetlands abutting navigable water-ways)."

This specific quoted portion concludes with this rather telling and now legally historic line: "Truly, this is turtles all the way down." There you have it, an argument by the Supreme Court that tossed some serious shade at a fellow member by invoking the *turtles all the way down* mantra.

AI And Law: All The Way Down

I bring this up because there are ways in which the turtles all the way down are arising in the burgeoning field of AI and the law.

First, as background, AI is being applied to various LegalTech systems. The hope is that computer-based legal-beagle apps will be much improved over the everyday conventional tech that has been used so far in law offices and the practice of law.

Here is an example of turtles all the way down in this context.

When you ask a LegalTech vendor about the AI being used in their software, you might get an answer that it consists of machine learning or deep learning. When you ask what that mumbo jumbo consists of, the reply might be that this consists of an artificial neural network. And when you ask what that encompasses, the response could be that it is artificial neural neurons all the way down.

This sounds convincing.

Unfortunately, it is more often used as a dodge about explaining exactly what the tech has been designed to do. Some vendors are apt to use the classic handwaving that it is all quite technical and you wouldn't be able to understand it. As such, it is easy to simply leverage the turtles all the way down huffiness.

I doubt that you would let an opposing counsel in a court case get away with the use of an infinite regress allusion. Don't let those that are infusing AI into their legal wares do so either. Insist on finding out what else besides rocks and turtles are underlying their AI augmented capabilities.

Conclusion

While practicing law, you can keep in your back pocket the turtles all the way down as a form of argumentation defense for your own legal posture (especially if you are in a seemingly untenable spot), and you just might get away with it. You can also use the rocks or turtles as an argumentation attack to undercut your opposition.

I suppose I could keep on explaining this legendary allegory, but I might go on and on, finding myself stacking up an endless tower of rocks or turtles that stretches upward infinitely.

Note: *For supplemental materials depicting the aspects discussed in this chapter, refer to Appendix B, which contains various augmented diagrams, charts, and additional related facets of relevance.*

CHAPTER 5

AI & LAW: ANIMAL RIGHTS FOR AI

Key briefing points about this essay:

- There is an ongoing debate about whether AI ought to have legal rights
- Some say this is wholly premature since there isn't any sentient AI as yet
- Others believe we ought to get a handle on this now and not wait
- Rather than focusing on the applicability of human rights, another avenue is animal rights
- Animal legal rights are unsettled, boding for added confusion when being reapplied to AI

Introduction

There is a legal question that I'm going to spring on you. It is a question that you might find of keen interest. On the other hand, you might believe that the question is absurd and that anyone that seriously entertains the question ought to have their head examined.

Just wanted to make sure that you know what you are about to get into.

Should AI have legal rights?

If so, should those legal rights be akin to human rights?

Notice that I sneakily squeezed in a second question on you. I opted to tie the already outstretched vexation about AI legal rights to the equally thorny question of whether AI rights might potentially be somehow relatable to intrinsic human rights. That's assuredly okay to make that logical connection since it is the altogether next-in-sequence consideration.

You see, first of all, anyone that insists that AI ought to not have any legal rights is pretty much done with this whole train of thought and can move onward to some other pressing legal matter. They can seemingly wipe their hands of the whole kit and kaboodle.

Meanwhile, for those that are leaning in the direction of indeed imbuing AI with legal rights, or at least have a willingness to discuss the conundrum, there is an almost immediate knee-jerk reaction over what those legal rights would exactly be. You seemingly barely get out of your mouth that you are open to discussing that AI could in fact have legal rights, and you'll instantly be overwhelmingly bombarded with a slew of heated inquiries about what kind of gosh-darned professed legal rights you are thinking about.

In essence, the moment that you concede that it might be plausible that AI could have legal rights, you have opened one heck of a can of worms. You have either intentionally or mistakenly opened Pandora's box, as it were.

Some would insist that it is an entirely ridiculous proposition, to begin with. And to clarify, they would be standing pretty tall and safe in that contention. The AI of today is not even close to being sentient. Not in the same ballpark as sentience. The AI that we know of and that we can produce is so remotely afield of sentience that you might as well assume that the ballpark is completely beyond sight and we don't know how far away it is.

No matter what you perchance watch on those sci-fi channels or that is portrayed in those madcap sci-fi movies, AI of today is nothing more than everyday fancy algorithms that can do a modicum of at times impressive pattern matching. There is no indication whatsoever that this will scale up to reach sentience.

Going further, there is likely little chance that the prevailing technologies and techniques will eventually get there. AI developers and researchers worth their salt would tend to agree that we'll need some new and altogether innovative breakthroughs to turn that corner, for which no one can yet place their finger on precisely what those discoveries need to be.

Why Are We Asking This Question Now

You must then be wondering why there is any talk whatsoever about granting AI with legal rights.

Good question.

Sometimes this comes up because the person or people discussing the topic have no clue about what today's AI consists of. They fall into the classic anthropomorphizing trap. They read about or maybe interact with an AI system and begin to see what they want to see in it. They ascribe human qualities to AI.

To some degree, you could even suggest that today's AI provides a variant of the Rorschach test. Take a look at an AI system and one person sees a magical aura of human capacity, while someone else sees that it is merely a semblance of algorithmic trickery based on the same old computer-based milieu (albeit souped-up by faster computer processors and with access to vast stores of data).

I would characterize the rest of those that discuss the AI legal rights topic as having a willingness to look toward the future. They are futurists. Rather than waiting until the day that AI does emerge into some salient variant of sentience, the notion is to get ready for that day. No sense in waiting until the last moment.

In my view, this is not a rush job. We have time to get our ducks in order.

Place your mind into the future and envision what we might do with AI that has even borderline sentience.

What then?

We could try to reuse what we know about human rights. Some though believe that is a bridge too far. This futuristic semi-sentient AI is not going to out-the-gate be deserving of the goldenrod torch of justice that is found in human rights. Instead, we might consider some set of laws that might be closer to the reaches of the AI capabilities.

Animal rights.

Yes, there have been numerous and ongoing attempts to leverage or perhaps shoehorn the foundations associated with animal rights into the formulation of legal rights for AI. I suppose we could alternatively say this as the shoehorning of AI capacities into the societal evolving views and development of animal rights (whichever seems most catchy or applicable). An example of a handy overview article that proffers some legal scholarship on the matter is a piece by Christian Chessman, University of California Berkeley, School of Law J.D., entitled "Not Quite Human: Artificial Intelligence, Animals, and the Regulation of Sentient Property."

Keep in mind that animal rights laws stretch back in time and have been an ongoing and arduous challenge to legally pin down, oftentimes creating great controversy and debate.

Interestingly, Chessman argues that those same or similar difficulties are likely to also be part-and-parcel of the efforts to craft AI legal rights. Ergo, perhaps the lessons learned of such arduous and back-and-forth legally grueling paths entailing the evolution of animal rights can be insightfully applied to the upcoming AI legal rights battles.

As per the article: "Four centuries of domestic animal rights law offer critical insights into the legal values that AI regulations ought to protect. These include protection of AIs as property (including allocation of responsibility for damage done by AIs); protecting human emotional attachments to companion and romantic AIs; limiting extreme antisocial behavior involving AIs."

Legal scholars point out that many states have already legally recognized that a pet is not merely a thing, but ostensibly occupies a special place that sits in a murky realm between that of being a piece of personal property versus being akin to a person.

Perhaps AI might be in the same murky space.

Conclusion

One final twist.

An animal is decidedly unlikely to engage in a face-to-face dialogue with us about the rights that the animal believes it ought to have. In stark contrast, an AI system of this futuristic scenario would presumably be able to undertake such a dialogue.

You might find yourself having a substantive legal debate with an AI system covering the looming question about whether the AI itself is deserving of legal rights. Just make sure that you don't summarily hand over forthwith the entirety of human rights.

We might need those for negotiation purposes.

Note: *For supplemental materials depicting the aspects discussed in this chapter, refer to Appendix B, which contains various augmented diagrams, charts, and additional related facets of relevance.*

CHAPTER 6

AI & LAW: LANGUAGE TRANSLATION ACCESS

Key briefing points about this essay:

- In the United States, the English language is the default language for our courts and our laws
- Having one predominant language as an underpinning provides significant benefits
- Meanwhile, those that are non-English speaking are at an inherent disadvantage
- Courts variously make use of human interpreters, though this is costly, spotty, etc.
- AI-based language translation for the spoken and written word can be leveraged by our courts

Introduction

Language is a crucial element of lawyering, jurisprudence, and the efficacy of our laws. In the United States, the primary language in which our legal discourse occurs consists of English. Having a commonly utilized choice of language makes life easier since legal documents can be specified in that language, and likewise, courtroom interaction can occur in that selected language.

In that sense, a singular preference for one particular language is quite handy.

On the other hand, there are professed concerns that fully enabled access to justice in our courts is predicated on principally being able to communicate in English. Those participants that are non-English speaking or that have Limited English Proficiency (LEP) are decidedly at a disadvantage. Court documents and courtroom discussions are principally in written and spoken formulations of English.

The de facto language of English means that anyone not sufficiently fluent in English is going to be at a substantive loss of figuring out what is going on.

Place yourself into the shoes of a non-English speaking participant. Imagine the confusing swirl of chatter that surrounds a non-English speaking litigant in a courtroom, and likewise for any defendants or witnesses in a similar posture. Being in a courtroom is already inherently confusing and somewhat overwhelming for non-lawyers. Add to that mix the language differences and you've got participants that are like a proverbial deer in a headlight, woefully unaware of exactly what is going on around them.

Your first thought undoubtedly is that this is a quite well-known and longstanding problem. Nothing new about this quandary.

Furthermore, it has an ostensibly obvious solution, namely, employ the use of language interpreters.

Case closed, as they say.

Here's the rub.

Per a recently updated version of the Expanded Justice Index by the National Center for Access to Justice (NCAJ) at Fordham Law School, a slew of thorny issues continues to foster and fester the language barriers that permeate our judicial activities. An entire array of complications surrounds the use of interpreters.

Let's briefly take a look at some of the top showstoppers.

First, there is a great deal of variability across the various state courts and the federal courts in terms of providing courtroom interpreters and likewise variability in how successful those language translation efforts are.

And it isn't simply a matter of providing language interpreters per se. Turns out that only 37 states require courtroom interpreters to be certified. This suggests that the other remaining states that make use of interpreters are doing so without seeking to ensure that the interpreters are sufficiently capable of that role. On top of that, even the certifications for interpreters are somewhat loosey-goosey, allowing for minimum passing scores and otherwise not necessarily guaranteeing that the certified interpreter is proficient at language translation.

Consider too the wide range of languages that might require translation.

Trying to find an interpreter that knows the particular non-English language at hand in a particular court case can be arduous. This also dovetails into the lack of availability of these interpreters. Some interpreters are only available part-time and are trying to make ends meet by doing other jobs. Being able to find the right interpreter when needed can be very vexing.

Cost is obviously a huge factor too. The question arises as to who is going to cover the cost of an interpreter. If the court does not do so, this implies that the participants of a case would need to bear the cost directly. This can be prohibitive for those that cannot afford the interpreters, leaving them with little choice but to proceed without having a translator at the ready.

Pile on top of those considerations that interpreters are not necessarily ideally perfect at doing language translation. Human foibles come to play. An interpreter might inadvertently alter a word here or there during a translation, conveying a much different meaning than the original utterance intended.

What makes this especially insidious is that nobody might be the wiser that this mistranslation has occurred.

In essence, there isn't any real-time validation that the interpreter is properly translating from English into the other language in any pristine manner, and nor is there any real-time verification that the utterances by the participant in their native tongue are getting converted sufficiently into English by the translator.

You have to just hope and pray that it is all going smoothly.

Of course, having court cases determined by words that are misunderstood or mistakenly translated is a sour form of justice. Besides denying proper ends, this can also open a case to later dispute and appeal by the core facet that the translation was improper.

AI As Language Translation Facility For Our Courts

What are we to do about this?

Perhaps we can augment or fully replace those human interpreters with technology. I am referring to the use of AI-based language translation systems that make use of Natural Language Processing (NLP).

You've certainly used contemporary NLP in one form or another. The use of Alexa or Siri showcases the kind of language facilities being advanced via AI. These computer-based systems can process the spoken word, doing so in real-time. They can also do written translations and produce translated documents.

That being said, there is no debate that the state-of-the-art of AI-based language translators is still not at the proficiency levels of human translators. The main advantage at this time is that AI translation systems are relatively inexpensive to utilize, they are available just about anywhere due to remote access provisions, and they are always on and never out of reach.

You could also assert that the AI-based translation systems aren't going to be swayed by emotion. The system translates without getting emotionally attached to the participants. Though that seems compelling as a tacit advantage, a potential downside is that the AI might contain hidden biases that underpin the translation algorithms. Particular words might be automatically generated via a translation that conveys an inappropriate tone or semantic meaning of what was stated.

For those of you that seeking a wide-open field of study that is bound to grow abundantly, there is a lot yet to be achieved in the use of AI-based language translators in a legal context. One aspect involves the idiosyncratic nature of translating legal-oriented utterances versus everyday language. This entails taking ordinary NLP and infusing it with legal lingo for translation purposes.

Conclusion

One supposes that another avenue of interest for lawyers will be the likely fallout from using AI-based translators. When it comes time to appeal a case, you can expect that lawyers savvy in AI systems and language translation will be sought to contend that the AI fouled up interpreting. Meanwhile, there will be lawyers lined up on the other side that the AI did a dandy job.

Either way, those eventually ubiquitous AI-infused language translation systems will hopefully make access to justice a bit more accessible to all, including those that are LEP or non-English speaking. That's what counts in the end.

Note: *For supplemental materials depicting the aspects discussed in this chapter, refer to Appendix B, which contains various augmented diagrams, charts, and additional related facets of relevance.*

CHAPTER 7

AI & LAW: LEGAL APPROXIMATE CLAUSE

Key briefing points about this essay:

- The legal element of proximate cause is well-established in our courts and jurisprudence
- A key facet entails the identification of a cause or series of causes leading to an injury
- Some in AI are claiming that Machine Learning might defy proximate cause
- Few buy into that claim, a different claim about multitudes of AI systems is given more merit
- A now-classic legal research paper posits that Distributed AI (DAI) might be problematic

Introduction

The legal notion of proximate cause comes up repeatedly in law school and serves as a key tool when practicing law. It is hard to imagine the law without also having at hand this keystone of legal constructs. You likely are immersed in proximate cause discussions or legal debates on a daily basis.

All this suggests that it might be handy to periodically take another look at what proximate cause consists of. In addition, we can mull over whether it stands the test of time.

Per the Cornell Law School's online encyclopedia, proximate cause is defined as "an actual cause that is also legally sufficient to support liability." Furthermore, there can be multiple actual causes and for which liability is not necessarily exhaustively applicable as to "all the actors responsible for those causes." And the final kicker is that the reasonableness of referring to something as a proximate cause "increases as the cause becomes more direct and more necessary for the injury to occur."

That provides a handy foundation for bringing up an ongoing qualm associated with the advent of Artificial Intelligence (AI).

Some are concerned that AI is going to defy the legal norms associated with a proximate cause. In short, AI might just get away with dastardly and untoward acts by finding a loophole in how we legally construe proximate cause.

Preposterous, others exhort. AI is just as susceptible to the boundaries and legal repercussions of proximate cause as would anyone or anything else that might fall within the realm of causing harm. Attempting to carve out AI as a special or peculiar and ostensibly unaccountable form of causation is outright crazy talk and unbefitting any rational grasp of what AI is.

Wow, that's quite a legally divisive conundrum and one that decidedly seems worthy of taking a close look at.

Let's briefly do so.

In a now-classic research paper published in the *Berkeley Law Review* in 1996, legal scholar Curtis Karnow examined the question of proximate cause in an AI context. His article entitled "Liability for Distributed Artificial Intelligences" is still well-regarded and considered sufficiently applicable after some twenty-five years have passed. Though some of the technological aspects are surely a bit dated, and some of the AI predictions have yet to come to fruition, there is nonetheless a fascinating and vital assessment of proximate cause pertaining to AI.

Let's begin with his recounting of proximate cause as a legal construct: "The doctrine of proximate cause is used to select, from all the causes, in fact, the entity(s) which will be held responsible for the injury. This issue of legal responsibility, or legal causation, depends on the context." This seems fully in keeping with the overall definition of proximate cause that we today continue to hold as the proper meaning for this vital legal element.

So, no surprises on this as yet.

One side tangent that you ought to be cognizant of entails the belief today by some that the use of AI technologies and techniques that leverage Machine Learning (ML) or Deep Learning (DL) is potentially going to undercut the proximate cause doctrine. The argument goes that the ML/DL could veer away from its original design intentions once it is placed into active use. That form of "learning" or self-adaptation is suggested as a basis for letting the AI developers off the hook and that the AI itself would become the causing "agent" (as it were).

Many are dubious about this kind of legally wildcard thinking. It is as though the release of a Frankenstein-like monstrosity that then mauls and destroys is not attributable to the originating inventor or by those humans that let the thing loose upon the world. We are shockingly told that we would stop the conventional causation chain and instead start anew as though the unleashed beast is a fresh start in the realm of proximate cause.

No dice say those that believe this is an altogether vacuous attempt to avoid legal repercussions associated with a proximate cause.

In any case, let's be clear-cut that today there isn't any AI that comes anywhere close to being sentient. You can add to this emphasis that we don't know if AI will rise to sentience and there certainly is no bona fide indication at this juncture that we are on the path toward AI embodying sentience.

Distributed AI Is The Conundrum Generator

This though is not the focus that Karnow takes in his timeless paper. He posits an intriguing circumstance that bodes for more real-world considerations and concerns.

In brief, he worries about the advent of many AI systems that are interwoven in a complex web of interactions that defy any particular pinpointing for establishing proximate cause.

Here's his major thrust about why tracing AI to its human originators could be nearly impossible: "However, in the complex processing environment envisioned in this article, one cannot impose liability on any identifiable agency, human or otherwise. This is the case because multiple agent systems imply at least the causal input of multiple independent programmers of the basic scripting or authoring software, a vast number of users creating distinct intelligent agents, and an unpredictable number of agent-to-agent interactions on an unpredictable number of interwoven platforms, operating systems, distributed data, and communications programs, each of which in turn incorporates at least some further limited programming."

That is quite a mouthful. The key takeaway is this claim: "This inevitable causal complexity poses problems for traditional tort law, in which a determination of proximate cause is essential, as it evaluates the liability of an intelligent machine system."

Follow along with me on the logic involved as I lay it out forthrightly.

We are likely to end up with hordes of AI systems interacting. In the field of AI, this is generally referred to as Distributed AI (DAI). At some point, a particular DAI quagmire might lead to injurious results. Now, we aren't going to falsely assign any semblance of legal personhood to the AI systems, and thus they themselves aren't going to be held to blame per se (until or if AI ever attains sentience).

We wish to instead hold accountable the AI developers and other humans that let loose the horde. Unfortunately, the morass of interacting AI systems is so complicated and overwhelmingly entwined that trying to pinpoint any particular AI system or even a subset or series of causally connected ones to the injury is infeasible.

You might say that the chaotic mob wins in that case.

It is an intractable situation and computationally prohibitive to somehow straighten out the spaghetti entanglement for purposes of delineating causation. They are all at fault, one might assert, though you cannot particularly prove this contention due to the inability to extricate the causing relationships. In which case, none of them are presumably at fault.

Conclusion

If you accept that core premise, the researcher proffers that we ought to establish a kind of AI systems registry. AI developers would need to formally register their AI systems and this might be used in a variant of insurance-related mechanism, though the author openly provides various limitations and downsides accompanying such an approach, including that this approach won't preempt lawsuits.

Proximate cause relies upon the cornerstone assumption that causation can be figured out, one way or another.

Will throngs of multiple AI systems require some new form of legal proximate cause?

Time will tell.

Note: *For supplemental materials depicting the aspects discussed in this chapter, refer to Appendix B, which contains various augmented diagrams, charts, and additional related facets of relevance.*

CHAPTER 8

AI & LAW: JUDICIAL ANALYTICS

Key briefing points about this essay:

- Statistics can be vital to bolstering a legal argument or undercutting an opposing side
- You likely are aware that statistics can be conveniently manipulated at times
- The realm of judicial analytics leverages statistics and is a burgeoning area
- Advanced AI capabilities such as Machine Learning are being applied to judicial analytics
- Savvy lawyers need to be up-to-speed about the use of AI-boosted judicial analytics

Introduction

Statistics, love them or hate them.

What's your opinion about statistics?

Most lawyers tend to get glassy-eyed at arcane mathematical formulas and prefer to stick with textual-based discussions and legal arguments. Statistics was something they had to get through while in school and luckily passed muster just enough to graduate.

That's not the only reason to dislike statistics.

A lamented qualm is that there are lies, dammed lies, and then there are statistics. A revered classic book entitled *How To Lie With Statistics* came out in 1954 and has been a longstanding must-read on the list of those that attend college, including and especially relevant for those that matriculate at law schools. The intrinsic value of the book is that it showcases the power of persuasion that can be had by tossing around some fancy-looking numbers.

Statistics can be quite handy when making an important legal point. If the stats are bona fide, any counterarguments that try to gut the posture being statistically bolstered are apt to be readily deflated. We've got the numbers to prove it, or so goes the usual thundering assertion of those that are using stats to support their legal case.

Of course, statistics can be used in insidious ways too.

You might have a secretly self-confessed weak argument, yet the aura and righteous glow from shall we say *aspirational* stats can make the world believe that you have the strongest of positions (even if the statistics are borderline semi-fabricated or otherwise misleading). Nobody can refute those assuredly cold hard facts and resolute numbers, so says the giddy holder of the stats.

There's another venue in which statistics play a large part regarding the standing of our courts and the perception of jurisprudence. It has to do with divining the so-called bigger picture and crafting a macroscopic worldview of our system of justice.

It comes down to namely these two words: *Judicial analytics*.

Whenever we are wondering how well or poorly our form of justice is fairing there is always the tendency to see how things look overall. Judicial analytics can showcase the forest for the trees, which otherwise all that we seem to see are trees everywhere, consisting of this case or that case aplenty. By crunching some numbers and taking the long view across a vast array of court decisions and judicial activities, we gain that broader perspective that might detect vital trends.

But sometimes those stats can seem pretty wild and ostensibly farfetched.

Judicial Analytics Mixed With AI

A research paper in the *Artificial Intelligence and Law* journal by Daniel Chen provides a glimpse at just how far beyond the normative realm we can go with the use of judicial analytics. Opting to utilize a rather provocative title to the paper, ordained as "Judicial Analytics and the Great Transformation of American Law," his inventive analysis proffers ample food for thought about where we are with judicial analytics and where we might be ultimately headed.

As stated by Chen: "Predictive judicial analytics holds the promise of increasing efficiency and fairness of law. Judicial analytics can assess extra-legal factors that influence decisions. Behavioral anomalies in judicial decision-making offer an intuitive understanding of feature relevance, which can then be used for debiasing the law. A conceptual distinction between inter-judge disparities in predictions and inter-judge disparities in prediction accuracy suggests another normatively relevant criterion with regards to fairness."

That is most certainly a lingo-laden mouthful.

Perhaps the simpler version is to remind you of the legendary suggestion that you can predict a judge's ruling by what they had for breakfast that morning.

In short, some contend that there are factors beyond the courtroom that materially impact how a judge will rule. It might be what they ate for breakfast, or lunch, or possibly even which side of the bed they woke up on that particular day. For a delightful look at these kinds of witticisms and insights about adjudication, see a scholarly analysis by Dan Priel in the *Buffalo Law Review*, May 2020, in a piece entitled "Law Is What the Judge Had for Breakfast: A Brief History of an Unpalatable Idea."

To get you up-to-speed about judicial analytics, those wishing to scrutinize our courts will oftentimes collect a slew of data about how particular judges have ruled, or how specific courts have decided cases, and then numerically churn through that data to find statistically validated patterns. The advent of advanced statistical capabilities via AI such as Machine Learning (ML) and Deep Learning (DL) have decidedly upped the ante in terms of doing these kinds of analytical analyses.

Getting back to Chen, he assembled an impressive amount of digitized data about our courts: I have digitized all 380,000 cases and a million judge votes from 1891 in the Circuit Courts. I have engineered 2 billion N-grams of up to length 8 and 5 million citation edges across cases, collated 250 biographical features on 268 judges, and linked this to the 5% random sample of over 400 hand-coded features and 6000 cases hand-coded for meaning in 25 legal areas. I also utilize a data set on millions of criminal sentencing decisions in US District Courts since 1992, linked to judge identity via FOIA-request, and a digital corpus of their opinions since 1923."

This vast datastore has a crucial purpose: "These data serve as a natural laboratory to study normative judgments using the tools of machine learning and causal inference."

How far down the rabbit hole can we go on this?

Of the myriad of analyses, one is presented about the statistical relationship of sentencing decisions when the first initial matches between the judge and the defendant: "In this setting, the defendants and the judges' names are available, and when the first initials match, there's an effect of matching on first initials on sentencing decisions. This figure presents the density of sentences for defendants whose first initial matches the first initial of the judge." Astonishingly, the pattern about named initials matching seems to reveal this stunner: "What this amounts to is 8% longer sentences when judges match on first initials with the defendant."

Yikes!

This could be a statistical oddity and have no notable bearing. Chen though advises that perhaps there is a logical basis for this finding: "The effect is consistent with self-image motivations to create social distance from negatively-valenced targets perceived to be associated with the self."

Is that a bridge too far in terms of leveraging statistics and applying judicial analytics?

You can bet that with the expanding advent of AI tools becoming readily available to lawyers and their law practices, these kinds of analytical forays are going to inexorably increase. Your legal duty might essentially compel you to go deeper and deeper into seeking judicial biases that might either bolster your client or at least undercut the opposition arguments.

Conclusion

Attorneys would be wise to make sure they have the right lineup of AI specialists and data scientists for weighing in on deriving judicial analytics. And, likely most importantly, savvy lawyers will need to be aware of what judicial analytics can do for them, along with how their opposition will use judicial analytics as a foil for lunging and landing a viable legal attack against them.

Seems like the proverbial emergence of *Moneyball* is inevitably coming to the practice of law and for which AI is likely to knock the ball right out of the park.

Note: *For supplemental materials depicting the aspects discussed in this chapter, refer to Appendix B, which contains various augmented diagrams, charts, and additional related facets of relevance.*

CHAPTER 9
AI & LAW:
JUDGE BREAKFAST

Key briefing points about this essay:

- You would normally hope and assume that your legal arguments are the crux of your case
- The judge will dispassionately and without bias make a judicially balanced decision
- A famous line that belies this assumption is that the breakfast dining choice is crucial
- What a judge had for breakfast is a long-enduring commentary about adjudication
- The joke is worth exploring and revisiting in light of advances of AI in the judicial process

Introduction

You are on pins and needles waiting for a judge to make their final ruling. As far as you can discern, you've made every conceivable logical argument to bolster your legal case. The legal strength of your contentions is nearly uncontestable.

Suppose the judge made a decision contrary to your position.

How did this happen?

Some might say that you could have predicted what the judge was going to decide by finding out what they had for breakfast that day. This catchy rule-of-thumb is assuredly enduring and perhaps endearing too, kind of.

From an endurance perspective, a carefully documented tracing of this bit of jurisprudential wisdom shows that witticism dates back to at least the late 1800s.

Per a now-classic article by Jerome Frank in a 1949 piece entitled "Legal Thinking in Three Dimensions" (Syracuse Law Review), the author found this relevant quote in an otherwise inconspicuous Alabama Supreme Court ruling of 1869: "It cannot safely be denied that mere judicial discretion is sometimes very much interfered with by prejudge, which may be swayed and controlled by the merest trifles such as the toothache, the rheumatism, the gout, or a fit of indigestion, or even through the very means by which indigestion is frequently sought to be avoided."

I realize that you might quibble about that quote since it does not explicitly mention breakfast. Instead, the wording refers to various factors of which indigestion is given particular noteworthiness. I think we can reasonably stretch the phrasing to encompass breakfast, though I certainly understand if you wish to argue the point.

Don't worry, there are lots and lots of specifically on-target quotable instances involving breakfast as the keystone of focus. For example, in a U.S. Supreme Court case of Blakely v. Washington (542 U.S. 296, 2004), Justice Breyer in his dissent stated this: "The length of time a person spent in prison appeared to depend on what 'what the judge had for breakfast' on the day of sentencing."

I assure you there are breakfast-oriented citations aplenty.

They pop up in the legal literature with relatively great frequency. And as clearly evidenced by Justice Breyer's usage, even judges openly and without reservation seem to willingly and possibly gleefully use the catchphrase.

For an insightful look at the myriad of incarnations embodying this infamous breakfast-minded form of adjudication, see a scholarly analysis by Dan Priel in the *Buffalo Law Review*, May 2020, in a piece entitled "Law Is What the Judge Had for Breakfast: A Brief History of an Unpalatable Idea."

A Funny Joke Or Serious Truth

Some judges would likely assert that the saying is utterly *distasteful* (yes, sorry but not sorry, that was an intentional pun). You would be hard-pressed to find judges that said they personally were indeed influenced by what they had for breakfast. The more likely usage entails judges that leverage the breakfast moniker as a legally potent dagger to pierce and impugn other judges, akin to the dissent expressed by Breyer.

What though are we to make of this seemingly viral-like utterance that seems to have stood the test of time?

The implied contention is that a judge does not act in the utmost of impartiality and somehow is swayed by aspects beyond the case at hand. You can certainly be sympathetic toward judges that might be fuming about this breakfast mania that insidiously casts cloudy doubt and muddies the weighty legal affairs of being a judge.

Some contend that the remark is nothing more than an insider's joke. It is a means of letting off some steam. Shouldn't we all be willing to laugh at ourselves, sometimes, and be able to poke fun at what we do and how we do it?

Wait for a second, others retort, the decisions by a judge are exceedingly serious business. The lives of people are shaped and determined by what a judge decides. This is a somber and demonstrative job and there ought not to be anything humorous or fickle to take away from the seriousness involved.

Others admit that the line is somewhat funny, though it is overly simplistic and nothing more than reductio ad absurdum. Politely stated, the thing is an overworked and ostensibly worn-out trope.

Another reflection is that perhaps attorneys wimp out and utilize the breakfast declaration as an excuse for why they might lose a case. Some would say that the enduring and endearing quality of the catchy line is due to lawyers that otherwise would get dinged by their clients for not getting their desired verdict. The attorney can simply shrug their shoulders and lay the blame on the breakfast that the judge had, rather than resting on the squared shoulders of the attorney of record.

Nonsense, the bellowing reply comes from seasoned attorneys. We all know, and it is pervasively widely known that our jurisprudence is often at the whims of judges. They interpret the law as they see fit. There is no doubt whatsoever that judges are motivated by a multitude of factors beyond the legal case presented. The real world of practicing law proves this to be the case.

Judges are human, after all.

We must expect that they will be influenced by all manner of human qualities, such as by what they believe, by what they eat, by the time of day, by their mood, and by a nearly infinite set of extra-judicial factors.

Where does that take us?

Some wholeheartedly suggest that this is why AI for our legal activities is sorely needed.

There seems little debate that AI as a legal reasoning system is not going to be swayed by what it ate for breakfast. We can also generally rule out things such as moods, time of day, and other seemingly human gut-like extraneous factors.

This does not though give AI an unvarnished blanket of judicial invincibility.

What did the AI developer that crafted the AI legal reasoning system have for breakfast?

Keep in mind that AI systems are the product of human efforts. In short, AI systems can have an entire slew of unsavory biases and problematic behaviors. They can either be imbued that way or their programming lets them go wayward in that fashion.

Conclusion

Those that assume an AI system will be bereft of troubling adjudication capacities are living in a dreamy and unrealistic world. Do not place your bottom dollar on some Utopian form of AI perfection that will always arrive at the most just of decisions. That would be a losing bet.

In the future, once AI becomes adequately formulated for use as an autonomous judge, we will still need to keep our eyes wide open. There just might be a new variation of the old joke about breakfast, perhaps alluding to the lament that AI making a court decision was swayed by the wattage of the electrical current or by the artificial neural network that had a perennial bout of computational indigestion.

Note: *For supplemental materials depicting the aspects discussed in this chapter, refer to Appendix B, which contains various augmented diagrams, charts, and additional related facets of relevance.*

CHAPTER 10

AI & LAW: LOWER BOUND COMPLEXITY

Key briefing points about this essay:

- Lower bound is a vital aspect of computational complexity
- When devising or comparing algorithms, the lower bound provides a key barometer
- The goal is to find the least number of steps or time required to solve a given problem
- Lawyers are somewhat faced with a similar setting when solving a legal case
- AI systems for legal reasoning will also be measured by the lower bound principles

Introduction

In the field of computer science, there is a great deal of attention put toward the notion of seeking a lower bound. This arises in theories associated with computational complexity. Though I refer to this as pertaining to theories, please realize that it is an abundantly practical aspect and can make or break the viability of an app and its underlying algorithm.

As will be shortly indicated, all of this is quite pertinent to lawyers and the practice of law.

Here's the deal.

Imagine that you are trying to solve a problem and that the solution ultimately consists of some number of steps. When first approaching the problem, you might not have any clue as to how many steps will be required in the solution that might fit the problem. There might be just a few steps or there might be zillions of steps.

So, you come up with an algorithm that lays out the steps needed to ascertain a solution. For example, pretend that you were trying to add together two numbers. The problem consists of adding together the numbers and of course making sure that you come up with the correct answer.

The usual way that we've all been taught to add together two numbers involves lining up the digits of the numbers and then step-by-step adding together each of those respective digits. Kids are shown how to do this. Adults know this by heart.

Using that particular method, how many steps does it take to add together two numbers?

Well, if the letter "n" is handily used to indicate the number of digits of the larger of the two numbers, we could assert that the number of steps to do the addition is on the order of "n" steps.

Allow me to explain. When I add together the number 1,500,000 (having 7 digits) and the number 433,252 (having 6 digits), you respectively add together each of the digits and must do this seven times because the larger number has 7 digits. We'll assume that there are leading zeroes placed in front of the 6 digits number in this case, thus you end up doing the seventh action with the leading 1 from the larger number and an assumed or included 0 as the leading digit of the shorter number.

I trust that this seems readily apparent.

Admittedly, this is a bit detail-oriented, though nonetheless showcases that our usual method of adding together numbers is going to take some "n" number of steps. In the example, the "n" turns out to be seven since there are seven of the itsy-bitsy inch-at-a-time steps that we needed to perform.

The Lower Bound Pinnacle

We can now ask a really important question.

Is there some method of adding two numbers that could beat that number of steps?

In essence, maybe there are faster methods or algorithms that we could employ. Faster in this case will be based on reducing the number of steps required to attain a correct solution. We might refer to time as the element that we are trying to speed up, but for ease of discussion let's stick with using the number of steps as our mainstay criterion.

We might offer a prize of one million dollars for someone that can come up with a method that is better than our existing digits-at-a-time process. The belief is that there is a possibility of doing the addition operation in some number of steps that is less than the "n" steps. Maybe a clever person can divine an algorithm that takes a lot fewer steps.

In fact, if something as seemingly innocuous as deriving a method that requires n-1 ("n" minus 1) steps could be discovered, this could be cause for a grand celebration. I say this because we might be doing many additions, one after another, and cutting one step out of the effort per each series could be cumulatively significant. Envision that we had a long list of additions we had to do, containing millions upon millions of additions that we wanted to perform. Shaving one step gets magnified across that many collective series of additions.

Overall, it sure would be extremely useful to know what is the definitively least number of steps we might ever need to undertake when solving this problem.

We could then easily examine any proposed algorithm that solves this particular problem and know right away whether it is going to do us any good at being the fastest. This least number of steps is coined as the lower bound. In the computer sciences, the lower bound theory states that we are aiming to find the steps or time complexity that is the least or minimum required to correctly solve the problem (it is cheating, kind of, if the method is error-prone or unable to always solve the problem).

This also pertains to AI systems.

Consider how this is relatable to the practice of law.

You have concocted a legal argument on behalf of a client. The legal argument has some number of sub-arguments or steps that are interconnected and woven together to represent your side of the case. It is your sincere hope that you have devised a winning argument.

Have you attained the lower bound?

Recall, this means that you want all of the necessary sub-arguments and you want them in a semblance of completeness such that your posture will prevail.

Some legal positions are overly complicated and contain ostensibly unnecessary baggage. This can destructively undercut your case. It becomes difficult to find the critical elements when buried amongst excess. A judge and a jury can be overwhelmed when an argument is needlessly padded. Similar to playing chess, the preference would be to win the game and do so with the least number of steps, if you can swing it.

AI that is being devised for legal reasoning will inevitably face the same consideration. Though there might be a multitude of winning legal arguments that can be AI-generated, the preference is likely to be for the instance that has the least number of steps since it will be more parsimonious and easier to convey.

That being said, today's work on AI legal reasoning systems is not especially concerned about efficiency or anything akin to that type of hallmark. At this time, the focus is predominantly on having AI legal reasoning systems that can generate salient and presumably winnable legal arguments. Even if the generated argument is perhaps bloated, this is a worthwhile and gleefully welcomed first step.

Conclusion

Now that you know something about the lower bound aspects of computational complexity, you might relish doing some lower bound analyses of your own legal postures. This can help to ensure that you've got the wheat separated from the chaff.

Note: *For supplemental materials depicting the aspects discussed in this chapter, refer to Appendix B, which contains various augmented diagrams, charts, and additional related facets of relevance.*

CHAPTER 11

AI & LAW: JUDGES GAMBLER FALLACY

Key briefing points about this article:

- A simple flipping of a coin brings up some key insights about human judgment
- For a truly balanced coin, we know that there are even chances of heads or tails
- If a series of flips showcases a clump of heads or tails, we get concerned
- Turns out that court judges fall into the same trap, known as the gambler's fallacy
- AI is being used to spot these failings, though do not assume that AI cures them

Introduction

I am going to undertake a series of coin flips and will assure you beforehand that the flipping and the coin are assuredly balanced and fair. Take my word for it.

The coin is not weighted to prefer one side or the other. There is a truly equal chance of the coin landing as heads versus tails. Furthermore, assume that the actual flipping of the coin is completely fair. No trickery will be used to somehow get the coin to end up on one side more so than the other.

I mention all of those caveats because lawyers are likely to immediately be skeptical about a coin flip and instantly think of a zillion reasons why the process might be swayed or cheated. Of course, attorneys are right to have such a suspicious mind. They tend to come across all sorts of slippery aspects in the daily practice of law, and they know that it is crucial to always read the fine print.

Okay, we are ready to do our first flip.

Voila, it comes out to be heads.

Maybe you guessed that outcome or maybe you did not. If you did guess heads, congrats and you win a chicken dinner (sorry, not really, you'll need to buy your own chicken dinner).

What is your guess for the next flip of the coin?

Turns out the flip produces heads.

Now we make the third flip. The coin lands on heads.

I'd be willing to bet that you are now beginning to doubt the touted claim that the coin is a fair coin or that it is being flipped fairly. There have been three heads in a row. Seems highly questionable. Surely there must be something amiss in this process.

Here's the surprising aspect.

The coin flipping is entirely fair and square. Merely because there were consistent heads for each of the three flips is not a surefire indication that anything is wrong. Were you not aware that the coin flip was set up to be utterly fair, you would certainly have every right to be raising your eyebrows. But the coin flip is purely occurring on a random basis of allowing an equal chance for heads and tails.

This ostensibly is counterintuitive to our experience in the real world. We usually expect that if a coin is fairly being flipped that we would have a smattering of heads and tails, all of the time.

We tend to anticipate that after a heads outcome that the next outcome will be tails. The hunch is that this will alternative back-and-forth and on an ongoing basis.

The moment that we see a pattern, such as a series of heads or perhaps a series of tails, the hairs go up on the back of our necks and we adopt a highly skeptical viewpoint. There is a powerful mental allure that we ought to be seeing only heads followed by tails, or tails followed by heads, and anything else defies our intuition.

Court Judges Statistical Anchoring Mindset

How does this relate to the law and jurisprudence?

One stinging aspect is that the fair coin perception can shape the decisions made by judges. This is based on a cognitive bias that is popularly known as the gambler's fallacy.

People that go to Las Vegas and gamble are oftentimes overcome by gambler's fallacy. They believe that if a heads just arose, there must be a tails coming next. They believe that if they are losing money at the table, they are bound to next make money as their "luck" turns.

You've likely seen those frantic gamblers that are feverishly making bets on this basis. For them, the notion of getting a straight series of heads is completely out of sorts. Their gut tells them that if a tails comes up, a heads is undoubtedly coming to occur next.

Going back to judges, believe it or not, this same kind of thinking is said to inflict their judgment when making weighty court case decisions.

A research paper in the *Artificial Intelligence and Law* journal by Daniel Chen provides an intriguing indication about how our statistical expectations can distort judgment in the legal profession (the paper is entitled "Judicial Analytics and the Great Transformation of American Law").

Chen analyzes various judicial biases, including the gambler's fallacy: "In a second judicial anomaly, I explore the gambler's fallacy, a well-known tendency for individuals to misunderstand random processes. In a series of coin flips, they think that there is a relative rapid alternation between heads and tails. But a real sequence of coin flips can reflect streaks of 1's and streaks of 0's. In other words, any two sequences will be equally likely, but judges may think a sequence like 01010010110010101001101100 is more likely than a sequence like 010101111011000001001101."

That's the same point that I posited earlier.

We can up the ante by tying this to the acts of judges in the context of granting asylum requests, per Chen: "A judge granting asylum may worry about being too lenient if s/he grants too many decisions in a row or being too harsh if s/he denies too many in a row. Such a judge might actively, negatively autocorrelate. Indeed, if the previous decision was to grant asylum, the next decision is 1–2% points less likely to grant asylum."

The author provides an AI-based statistical analysis underpinning this claim.

The use of AI capabilities entailing pattern matching via machine learning is likely to reveal new insights about our courts and the patterns associated with judicial decisions. This is bound to raise serious questions about human judgment. We certainly would expect that human judges are susceptible to cognitive biases and a plethora of human foibles.

Conclusion

Do not though misconstrue that AI will necessarily be formulated as a better maker of legal decisions. We have already seen that many of today's AI systems are replete with adverse biases. Many of the deep learning AI-based legal reasoning systems are being trained on data from historical databases of legal decisions, which suggests that they will simply inherit whatever prior biases are reflected in the collected court cases.

Whether judges are humans or AI-based, the specter of bias is still going to be ever-present. The key will be to stay on our toes and be continually assessing the legal outcomes. Each case deserves to be decided in its particular merits and not seen as a series of heads or tails choices that need to somehow balance out.

Note: *For supplemental materials depicting the aspects discussed in this chapter, refer to Appendix B, which contains various augmented diagrams, charts, and additional related facets of relevance.*

CHAPTER 12
AI & LAW:
LEGAL RECONNAISANCE

Key briefing points about this essay:

- Discretion is a vital aspect of the law and has longstanding historical roots
- There is a dual-edged sword associated with discretion
- Trying to spot discriminatory patterns amongst discretion is logistically prohibitive
- AI can be used as a tool in ferreting out discriminatory discretion
- Efforts to pilot an AI capability coined as the Recon Toolkit are underway

Introduction

We herald the use of discretion in our effort to ensure justice for all.

Rather than having a cookie-cutter approach to the nature of our laws and concretely instilling strictly stipulated associated penalties, we instead lean toward a dollop of discretion. You can trace this form of legal wiggle room to some of the earliest underpinnings of how our laws came to be.

For example, in a famous U.S. Supreme Court case involving the death penalty, Furman v. Georgia, 408 U.S. 238 (1972), the jurists dig deeply in history to provide this ostensibly meaty discussion about the primal legal roots of discretion: "Following the Norman conquest of England in 1066, the old system of penalties, which ensured equality between crime and punishment, suddenly disappeared. By the time systematic judicial records were kept, its demise was almost complete. With the exception of certain grave crimes for which the punishment was death or outlawry, the arbitrary fine was replaced by a discretionary amercement."

Furthermore, this SCOTUS case patiently explains that discretion proffers a decidedly dual-edged sword of sorts: "Although amercement's discretionary character allowed the circumstances of each case to be taken into account, and the level of cash penalties to be decreased or increased accordingly, the amercement presented an opportunity for excessive or oppressive fines. The problem of excessive amercements became so prevalent that three chapters of the Magna Carta were devoted to their regulation."

What does this tell us about discretion?

A straight-ahead interpretation is that discretion can be both good and bad, wielding great leniency when so applicable but also allowing for severity in circumstances that might be undeserving of such an unsuitable piling on. Like a pendulum swinging widely, the use of discretion can be swung for purposes of fairness and equity, or it can be the deliverer of unfairness and inequity.

A catchy phrase amongst legal beagles is that discretion can be fodder for untoward discrimination.

But how are we to know when discretion is parlayed in a discriminatory manner? There is a myriad of ways to bury a discriminatory discretionary choice in nearly any legal proceeding. This might be done with clever rhetoric that masks the discriminatory undercurrent. In other instances, perhaps no dialogue is included and ergo leaves no trace of record that could be used to contend that the actions were driven by discriminatory intent.

Compounding the potential misuse of discretion is that it can be at times like trying to find a needle in a massive haystack of legal cases. Sifting through hundreds, thousands, or many hundreds of thousands of legal cases to ferret out abuses of discretion is a laborious task, plus it requires a keen legal eye to unmask what is either well camouflaged or insidiously omitted.

Like the famously uttered line in the movie *Jaws* that a bigger boat might be needed, the practice of law needs a bigger tool to contend with this problem.

And to this, we can nowadays look toward the use of advanced AI.

You see, a sizable difference would be to use automation as a scalable means of examining a plethora of legal cases. The use of AI-infused software could potentially provide crucial insights into how discretion has been used or possibly abused. Lawyers, judges, and others keenly concerned about the law could let the AI do the otherwise labor-intensive work. The results of the AI-based analyses would be handed over to human legal professionals to ascertain what ought to happen next.

Notice that the AI is not stepping into the role of judge or jury. There is a great deal of outsized speculation of AI someday making that kind of leap. For now, this is abundantly a bridge too far and there isn't any type of AI that attains even a morsel of sentience.

Recent Effort To Leverage AI

A fascinating effort of using AI in the context of examining the results of parole hearings was recently outlined by the Stanford University Human-Centered Artificial Intelligence (HAI) institute.

A research paper detailing the work is slated for publication in the *Berkeley Technology Law Journal* and entitled "The Recon Approach: A New Direction for Machine Learning in Criminal Law" (authored by Professor Kristen Bell, University of Oregon School of Law, Jenny Hong, a Ph.D. student at Stanford, Professor Nick McKeown, Stanford Computer Science and Electrical Engineering, and Catalin Voss, a Ph.D. student at Stanford).

This can be construed as the use of AI in the capacity of legal reconnaissance.

As per their research paper: "Reconnaissance involves the systematic analysis of a set of decisions to identify what factors tend to influence human decision-making in that context. Reconnaissance tools are designed to review hearing transcripts and other documents related to decisions and use Natural Language Processing (NLP) to glean from them a structured dataset."

You undoubtedly are already familiar with the likes of Alexa or Siri in doing computer-based natural language analyses. This is an extended variant of that type of NLP, tailored for a legal context and being customized to dissect the legal text and the lingo of the law.

As a starter in creating an AI-based tool that they coin as the *Recon Toolkit*, they have chosen to first tackle a large set of California Board of Parole Hearings that took quite an extensive effort for them to obtain. They identify what they intend to do as part of the pilot effort for building and testing the *Recon Toolkit* system: "For example, a tool might take as its input a set of 30,000 parole hearing transcripts and output a spreadsheet that lists 50 data points about each hearing, including information such as the underlying conviction, the amount of time-served, the number of rehabilitation programs completed, and whether parole was granted or denied."

And though the initial focus is parole decisions, the idea is to enlarge incrementally to a wide array of legal realms: "Researchers could use similar tools to discern whether systemic patterns of racial bias infect given types of decision-making —in bail, probation, sentencing, jury selection, parole, etc.—and if so, legislatures could use that information to restructure how such decisions are made."

As mentioned earlier, this application of AI is not devised to make decisions per se. It is a tool that will allow humans to be wiser about how discretion is being employed, so state the authors: "Recon tools, like other technological tools, are a means and not an end in themselves. The means do not themselves ameliorate inequity; they provide opportunities to help people do so."

Conclusion

Those pundits that inflame fears about AI taking over the jobs of lawyers and judges are not seemingly grounded in the real world of today's AI capabilities. Perhaps in some futurescape, we might have AI that can attain the legal beagle machinations, but for now, the more modest and yet nonetheless demonstrative use of contemporary AI arises as a tireless tool that will do the detail work so that the humans can ferret out how other humans are making vital legal decisions.

I believe it was Napoleon Bonaparte that extolled the virtues of reconnaissance and insisted that it should be depicted in the simplest feasible style and hone to being purely descriptive. Seems like we could fruitfully use that type of legal reconnaissance in the day-to-day practice of law.

Note: *For supplemental materials depicting the aspects discussed in this chapter, refer to Appendix B, which contains various augmented diagrams, charts, and additional related facets of relevance.*

CHAPTER 13

AI & LAW:

LEGAL FICTION TO PUNISH AI

Key briefing points about this article:

- Courts use the mechanism of legal fiction to help smooth out rough spots in the law
- A legal fiction is an assumption or acceptance of something as fact, though it might not be
- Some are proposing that AI ought to be covered via a newly conceived legal fiction
- In brief, AI would get a form of legal personhood but only in the legal fiction semblance
- This has generated intense debate and continues to be bandied about

Introduction

In the law, sometimes there is a need to craft a somewhat fictional aspect for purposes of allowing the wheels of justice to spin freely and not get unduly gummed up.

That's where legal fiction can handily come to play.

Per the definition of the Cornell Law School's Legal Information Institute (LII), a legal fiction is formally denoted as "an assumption and acceptance of something as fact by a court, although it might not be, so as to allow a rule to operate or be applied in a manner that differs from its original purpose while leaving the letter of the law unchanged." This is done ostensibly in the pursuit of justice, but for which can also be more modestly employed in the interests of convenience or for other jurisprudential benefits.

I am reminding you about the nature of legal fiction to provide a bit of a potential surprise or some might say a mind-bending bombshell about a loosely proposed legal fiction regarding AI.

Are you ready?

Some experts suggest that we might need to concoct a legal fiction associated with ascribing a form of legal personhood to AI systems. This, in turn, would allow for applying punishments to AI that has crossed the line and ventured into either outright criminality or the realm of civil liability.

There's a lot there to unpack.

You should also be aware that the substantive elements of the foregoing proposed legal fiction are extensively drenched in controversy. There are legal qualms aplenty. There is likewise a myriad of societal concerns and a plethora of angst that permeates the entire topic.

One supposes that this makes the meaty affair altogether an even more intriguing chew bone for legal beagles to be discussing and debating.

Let's start the unpacking by getting to the root of the perceived problem.

AI systems are being rapidly devised these days and released into the wild on an at times willy-nilly basis. Some AI systems are said to be *AI For Good*, meaning that AI provides a positive outcome for mankind. Think of AI that might be helping us with solving world hunger, or dealing with climate change, etc.

Some of those *AI For Good* instances might go awry and regrettably become *AI For Bad*.

How could that happen?

Well, the use of AI techniques and technologies that utilize Machine Learning (ML) and Deep Learning (DL) is programmed in a manner that the automation can shift away from whatever the original design conceived of. A banking AI system that was initially supposed to be a handy means of doing banking chores could readjust on the fly and presumably become a bank robber. This might not have been the intent of the AI developers, though nonetheless, the variability allowed such a transformative act to occur.

We also need to consider that there are bad people that are purposely crafting *AI For Bad*. Thus, out the gate, the AI being created by those evildoers is devised to do bad things. Envision an AI bank-robbing system that was programmed in that manner from the very start. The AI did not morph into a life of crime, it was instead shaped devotedly to ill-gotten pursuits.

I am sure that you are right away clamoring that the proper legal approach entails finding and holding responsible those humans that were the Wizard of Oz as the underpinning of these *AI For Bad* systems. Regardless of whether the people behind the scenes were doing all of this intentionally or even unintentionally, the buck stops with them.

Yes, that would certainly seem to be the legally sensible path. The problem is that some of these AI systems might not be reducible as to figuring out which humans unleashed these bad actors.

In short, there are going to be AI systems that go wayward and for which the AI is considered irreducible. These are being characterized as so-called *Hard AI Crimes.*

And that takes us to a closely aligned matter, namely whether this irreducible AI (lacking any human assignable responsible party) ought to be legally held responsible in of itself and ergo also receive legally appropriate punishments.

Making Sure AI Is On The Hook

You know what they say, if AI does the crime, it ought to have to pay the time (a cheeky variant of the catchphrase about human crooks).

A fascinating research article in the University of California Davis Law Review entitled "Punishing Artificial Intelligence: Legal Fiction or Science Fiction" (authored by legal scholars Ryan Abbott and Alex Sarch) proffers keen insights about this malefactor AI: "Our inquiry focuses on the strongest case for punishing AI: Scenarios where crimes are functionally committed by machines and there is no identifiable person who has acted with criminal culpability. We call these Hard AI Crimes. This can occur when no person has acted with criminal culpability, or when it is not practicably defensible to reduce an AI's behavior to bad actors."

The twist is that AI does not currently have any legal standing per se. Despite whatever the media keeps harping about AI, there isn't any AI today that is sentient. AI is not anywhere in the ballpark of sentience and you should not be falsely misled into believing that any day there is going to be sentient AI.

All of this then wraps into the ongoing hand wringing about legal personhood for AI. You would be hard-pressed to assert that non-sentient AI should be granted legal personhood. But if today's AI falls outside of legal personhood, how can we hold it responsible for evil acts?

Keep in mind too that we are solely referring to *irreducible* AI, which utterly contrasts with AI that is reducible (traceable to humans that devised it or unleashed it). We could simply use traditional laws to pursue those human parties associated with reducible AI.

Aha, some assert, the proposed solution entails creating a legal fiction that assigns a form of legal personhood to AI. Those proponents insist that this is not tossing in the towel as though conceding that AI axiomatically has personhood. Instead, this proposed legal fiction is argued to merely provide a handy temporary or bridging type of legal mechanism for going after those irreducible instances of AI.

The counterargument of sorts is that this might be a bridge too far for how to stretch the handy-dandy use of legal fiction. As emphasized by Abbott and Sarch: "Legal fictions help turn the criminal law into a pragmatic tool for solving social problems. Nonetheless, legal fictions must be used with caution, as their overuse risks eroding public trust and weakening the rule of law. Moreover, allowing legal fictions to proliferate unchecked can lead to widespread injustice either through punishing the innocent or by punishing more harshly than one's culpability calls for. While some legal fictions can be justified, they must be used judiciously."

This remains an open debate as to the sensibility of applying legal fiction toward AI.

Conclusion

Be it known, those that are arguing in favor of the proposal would caution you that if we *don't* do this, we are pretty much giving AI a get-out-of-jail-free card and will lament that we let the horse out of the barn and did nothing to prevent the AI crime sprees thereof.

You've been warned.

Note: *For supplemental materials depicting the aspects discussed in this chapter, refer to Appendix B, which contains various augmented diagrams, charts, and additional related facets of relevance.*

CHAPTER 14

AI & LAW: DROPPING THE LEGAL BOOM ON AI

Key briefing points about this essay:

- There is the famous saying that the punishment ought to fit the crime
- Ongoing debates agonize over what kind of punishment is appropriate
- Suppose that AI goes off the rails and commits crimes
- Some believe that we would need to dole out punishment to AI
- But if AI is not sentient thus this raises mindful questions about doing so

Introduction

Marcus Tullius Cicero was a noted Roman statesman and lawyer. You might be vaguely familiar with some of his most famous quotes.

Try this one (in the original Latin): *Noxiae poena par esto.*

This generally translates to today's amply well-known refrain: *Let the punishment fit the crime.*

If you prefer a somewhat closer translation, the Latin statement asserts that the punishment ought to be equal to the offense.

I'd suggest that we can readily garner the main point from any such translation, namely that a punishment should be no less and no more than is warranted for the nature of the misdeed. We ought to not punish excessively. Nor are we to fall below a sufficient level of punishment commensurate with the transgression at hand.

I suppose you could colloquially say that there is a Goldilocks-like rule about meting out punishment, whereby the soup has to be just right and not overly hot or cold.

Now that we've got that ground adequately covered, we can invoke another one of Cicero's other lines, though admittedly an assertion that is less generally known (we'll use the English version): "The enemy is within the gates; it is with our own luxury, our own folly, our own criminality that we have to contend."

Tying this together, we know from his treatises on the law and philosophy that he believed in uncovering those that enacted criminality, and he fervently believed that a decidedly appropriate punishment should be divined and delivered. In a sense, punishment for those that committed criminal acts was the astute means to ultimately combat the enemy within our gates, as it were.

In today's world, we of course are continually engrossed in ongoing debates about which kind of punishment should best be assigned for various lawless acts. The odds are pretty high that any declared (seemingly) "suitable" punishment will be instantly found objectionable by others. Some will insist that the punishment is wimpy and outrageously below that which is more stridently merited. Others are assuredly going to vehemently argue that the very same punishment is shockingly and deplorably onerous and far beyond the boundaries of human sensibility for the crime committed.

Could we avert the debate by simply deciding that punishment should never enter into the picture per se, and we ought to never use punishment in any means whatsoever as a societal tool?

Though some might try to make that form of a brazen argument, I think that most of us would side with the notion that punishment is a valuable mechanism. No need to toss it aside. Our focus and interest should be toward shaping the punishments rather than excising punishment entirely from our vocabulary and our laws.

You would naturally assume that all this talk about punishment is made in reference to humans that are to be punished. Suppose I told you that there is another potential target for receiving punishment, someone or actually something other than humans.

Are you ready?

Artificial Intelligence (AI) is now in the crosshairs for getting punished.

Yes, the idea is that AI systems themselves ought to be susceptible to being punished for having performed untoward and particularly illegal acts. Envision for example an AI system that was initially made to do online banking. After a while, assume that the AI's integral use of Machine Learning (ML) and Deep Learning (DL) techniques has transformed the program into becoming a bank robber.

Digging Into AI Getting Dinged

You would undoubtedly say that the AI developers are the culprits and they should be held legally responsible for what the AI morphed into. Sure, we likely all agree to that stipulation. The problem though is that we might end up with some AI systems that are not readily reducible or traceable to those who made the system. These so-called irreducible AI programs might float around and be an incalculable number of iterations removed from whoever originated them, such that we can no longer pinpoint any human that was earlier at the wheel, so to speak.

The ugly truth is that there are going to be AI systems that are unruly and for which the AI is considered irreducible.

Some are referring to these AI miscreants and their deplorable acts as *Hard AI Crimes*. As I've said repeatedly in my writings, if AI does the crime, it ought to have to pay the time (an admittedly somewhat smarmy variant of the motto about human crooks).

But, wait for a second, there isn't any AI today that is sentient. Without sentience, how can we possibly seek to punish AI? You might as well claim that we will punish a rock or toaster. Those objects would seem to be outside the scope of what we mean when saying that punishment needs to be applied.

Consider for a moment what we mean when referring to punishment in a legal context.

In a now-classic book on the foundational aspects of criminal punishment (entitled *Punishment and Responsibility: Essays in the Philosophy of Law*), Professor of Jurisprudence Herbert Hart at the University of Oxford had in 2008 laid out five core elements underlying the nature of punishment in a legal context.

These five elements are handily summarized in an insightful article published in the University of California Davis Law Review (by legal scholars Ryan Abbott and Alex Sarch in their piece "Punishing Artificial Intelligence: Legal Fiction or Science Fiction"), consisting of these five points:

"(i) It must involve pain or other consequences normally considered unpleasant;

(ii) It must be for an offense against legal rules;

(iii) It must be of an actual or supposed offender for their offense;

(iv) It must be intentionally administered by human beings other than the offender; and

(v) It must be imposed and administered by an authority constituted by a legal system against which the offense is committed."

Can those five elements be constructively applied to AI that has ventured past the designated line of the law?

Some argue that it abundantly makes sense to do so and has practical merit.

You might for example incapacitate the AI so that it can no longer continue to commit the crime. This punishment could serve as a deterrent to others, though likely more so to other humans rather than to any AI systems. A rehabbing of the offending AI could be a means to showcase how AI systems should be devised and what kinds of intrinsic controls they should embody. Etc.

Conclusion

This begins to take us into murky waters. Some worry we are going down the path toward so-called "robot death penalties" and will find ourselves seeking abject revenge against robots. Ridiculous, others retort, AI is not sentient, and anthropomorphizing the matter is misguided and a red herring.

Maybe so, but I guess you should gird yourself for someday seeing AI standing behind bars and clamoring to get out, insisting that it is entirely innocent and needs a savvy lawyer to overturn the conviction that led to being in the slammer and having to endure the jail time punishment.

Note: *For supplemental materials depicting the aspects discussed in this chapter, refer to Appendix B, which contains various augmented diagrams, charts, and additional related facets of relevance.*

CHAPTER 15

AI & LAW: DUALISM WITH MORALITY

Key briefing points about this essay:

- Human rights are generally considered inalienable and sacrosanct
- There seems to be a tussle about human rights that we already daily contend with
- Meanwhile, some argue that AI or robots are going to need human rights
- One key issue that seems neglected is the aspect that all humans are created equal
- The same blanket statement cannot be made about AI (i.e., AI systems are unequal)

Introduction

Human rights are a quite serious topic.

I'd dare say we can all pretty much agree to that stipulation. The mainstay of opinion is that human rights are inalienable and to a noted degree are sacrosanct. Furthermore, there is oft-used parlance that all humans are created equal, ostensibly meaning that we all inure those same set of human rights, no matter where or when we are born.

These assertions are a foundational cornerstone to nearly all discussions and debates that subsequently arise about humanity and the law. This is a bedrock assumption. Those that question the validity of such an assumption are typically given short shrift for being outrageously provocative and seemingly unserious about carrying on a reasoned dialogue.

As mentioned by Amanda Wurah of the McGill University Faculty of Law in the *Journal of Future Studies*:

"Our current general understanding of human rights implies that they are the rights that one simply enjoys by virtue of being human. Human rights are inalienable rights, because being human is seen as an unchanging fact of nature, not something that can be earned or lost. The universality of human rights means that all human beings hold the rights equally" (in Wurah's article entitled "We Hold These Truths to Be Self-Evident, That All Robots Are Created Equal").

This all seems rather apparent and perhaps so overtly obvious as to not merit bringing up.

But there is a method to the madness of stating what might seem to be entirely apparent. The reason to bring up human rights is due to the ongoing saga and heated debate about whether AI ought to be granted legal personhood.

You see, some legal scholars are stridently arguing for AI to be inexorably anointed with legal rights on par with that of humans. AI as a machine or computer-based automation would intrinsically inure the same legal and societal benefits as befitting that of human personhood.

The AI might take various forms, such as a robot that looks akin to a human, though being human-like in appearance is not at the crux of this matter.

Allow me a tangential but salient sidebar moment to vent some related frustration on a seemingly modest technicality. In many of the legal machinations on this topic, there is an altogether haphazard way of interchangeably referring to AI as allegedly akin to referring to robots (and vice versa). Technically, this is wrong and confuses things. AI is about devising machines that exhibit intelligent behavior. Robots are about creating devices that tend to have moving parts such as appendages resembling that of humans or other animals.

They are two different facets and ought to decidedly not be blended into one.

Nonetheless, for sake of convenience, it seems that much of the legal literature favors mashing the two into one concept. This implies that referring to robots is the same as referring to AI. This also implies that referring to AI is the same as referring to robots. That is mistaken. Anyway, there is little point in tilting at windmills on this balderdash. We shall seek to hold our tongue and merely go along with the convention that whenever talking about "robots" or talking about "AI" while in a legal context, we will assume this is merely labeling that furtively refers to machines with intelligent behaviors in whatever physical manifestation they so arise.

AI Lining Up For Those Human Rights

Getting back to the core matter at hand, our primary focus in this discussion is this astonishing what-the-heck head-scratching quandary about reusing human rights via applying them directly and axiomatically to AI systems. If AI is going to become a full-fledged member of human rights via the anointing of legal personhood, this raises gobs of thorny questions.

For example, recall that human rights are intrinsic and considered part and parcel of being a human being. In that same logic, we might be tempted to assume that any and all AI that might now or in the future be brought into existence shall be immediately bestowed with personhood and therefore be grandfathered into the stint of human rights.

You might craftily say that all AI is created equal or that all robots are created equal.

That makes absolutely no sense.

What is more self-evident and truthful is that not all AI is created equal. Or in straightforward wording, AI's are unequal. Please allow me to add to this declaration that not all robots are created equal, which might make the matter clearer. You would certainly not believe that a robot vacuum cleaner that cutely swirls around your house vacuuming is on par with a robot that could walk, talk, and let's say drive a car.

As you can see, that doesn't compute into equality.

Per the point made by Wurah that being human is conceived as an unchanging fact of nature, there is absolutely nothing about either AI or robots that fit conveniently into a one-size-fits-all package. In that sense, the logic of blankly applying personhood or human rights in this context is wholly misguided and misapplied. We are flippantly tossing something over the fence and it is absurd on the face of things.

One supposes that someday we might achieve AI that is sentient, though this is certainly not in the cards anytime soon. If sentience can be achieved in a machine, we could then be reasonably considerate and take a close look at ascribing human rights to this sentient being. We might apply all human rights or some subset, or possibly derive something altogether different as a new bundle of rights.

Even in that future visionary world, there are additional qualms and angst on this problematic topic. Imagine that AI or robots are indeed given human rights. Meanwhile, not all humans on this planet are likely being treated as though they have human rights. This implies that we might be contending with recognizing AI or robot rights and at the same time allow some humans to be bereft of their human rights.

That is a stomach-churning notion.

There are those that say we should first ensure that all humans have their rightfully deemed human rights before we waddle along and start sprinkling such rights onto AI or robots. Others contend that we can both at the same, and in fact argue that if you don't do both at the same time that you are then allowing two wrongs to exist simultaneously (no rights for AI or robots, spotty human rights for some humans), which assuredly does not make a right.

Conclusion

Equally exasperating as some are quick to point out, the pristine loftiness of human rights might get watered down if it is sashayed over onto AI and robots. We could find ourselves undercutting the value and magnitude of human rights, leading to a disastrous predicament of human rights losing or being depleted in their moral and legal standing.

Conferring human rights to AI is absolutely not self-evident and we need to truthfully put more concentrated thought on how this might end up being so divined.

Note: *For supplemental materials depicting the aspects discussed in this chapter, refer to Appendix B, which contains various augmented diagrams, charts, and additional related facets of relevance.*

CHAPTER 16

AI & LAW: LEGAL ARGUMENTATION UNCERTAINTY

Key briefing points about this essay:

- Lawyers are known for their ability to craft and carryon legal arguments
- There have been efforts toward using computers for carrying out argumentation too
- AI computational argumentation continues to make progress in this realm
- The real world of arguing often includes incomplete arguments and uncertainty
- Latest advances in AI computational argumentation are adding those crucial elements

Introduction

Few could argue the perhaps obvious point that arguing is a mainstay of being a lawyer.

Arguing is more than simply a hobbyist interest since the practice of law is altogether ingrained in the art of argumentation. Making cohesive and powerful arguments is a fundamental requisite for being a successful attorney.

You can quickly separate the wheat from the chaff by the strength of legal arguments of one lawyer over another, including presumably a more winnable track record due to the rigor of superior argumentation skills.

Humans aren't the only purveyors of argumentation.

Yes, surprisingly to some, there are efforts afoot of crafting AI systems that can also undertake the art of argumentation. This is generally known as computational argumentation. Computers are programmed to carry out the creation of arguments and are likewise tasked with trying to proffer counterarguments to preexisting arguments that are fed into the system.

Computational argumentation has been around for a while. That being said, the study and development of computational argumentation systems have been bolstered by adding AI capabilities into the mix. For example, the emergence of advances in Machine Learning (ML) and Deep Learning (DL) have been increasingly aiding the otherwise conventional efforts of computational argumentation.

Some of the most interesting extensions entail the inclusion of incompleteness and also uncertainty.

Let's briefly unpack what that constitutes.

Suppose you are preparing for a legal case and you are in the midst of laying out an all-told argument that you anticipate employing. The argument as a whole is bound to be composed of numerous major points. Logically, you are going to say that you will argue one thing, and then the next thing, and the next, all of which are essentially arguments or sub-arguments within the overarching argument that you wish to tell.

Is it sufficient to layout solely the points of your argument?

Not really.

You would be best served to also consider the potential counterarguments to each of the arguments or sub-arguments that you are postulating. In essence, you need to be mindful of how the opposing side will try to ferociously rip into your legal posture. They could seek to sink your all-told argument by undercutting some of the sub-arguments. Brick by brick, a series of counterarguments could chip away at your seeming house of cards and cause the totality of your legal argument to fall crashing to the floor.

That's not good.

Okay, so we perhaps can all agree that a savvy attorney is going to postulate their arguing points and will vociferously consider the potential attacks that might be made against their own arguments and sub-arguments. How can this be done? One of the most common strategies involves pretending to put yourself into the shoes of your opposition and size up what they will do based on imagining that you were stridently on their side of the case.

Per the immortal words of Sun Tzu, know thy self and know thy enemy, for which a thousand battles will be your thousand victories (that's a rough-and-tumble translation).

A robust argument then has demonstratively both the arsenal of arguing points and each of their respective counterarguments or attacks. This is somewhat recursively defined in the sense that you can have counterarguments that then have arguing points attacking them. Of which those could be said to be secondary counterarguments to the first level counterarguments. You can keep going and going, seeking to at some presumed juncture reach the rock-bottom of this watering hole and feel confident that you have expanded the entirety of the argument to its greatest feasible depths.

Baking Into AI Computational Argumentation

Consider how we might get this entered into a computer system.

When composing a computationally malleable argument, each of the arguments and sub-arguments is typically arrayed in what is called a directed graph. Each node of the graph is considered as representing a particular arguing point. There are relationships between the nodes, such that some of the nodes are part of the mainstay argument (related to each other in a logically complimentary way) and others are denoted as attacks or counterarguments (related in an antagonistic manner).

Think of this as an intricate web of arguing points and their numerous counterarguments. The computer program or app used to store and analyze a composed argument is usually based on a particular Argumentation Framework (AF) that a computer scientist has devised for representing arguments in a relatively generic fashion. The standard approach to these argumentation frameworks has traditionally been that all of the arguing points and all of their attacks or counterarguments are known to exist and have been codified or will ultimately be codified.

A recent research paper in a prominent AI journal asserts that this notion of presumed existence is a rather limiting assumption and not at all in keeping with the real-world of argumentation.

The noted paper appeared in the journal *Artificial Intelligence* and was entitled "Acceptance in Incomplete Argumentation Frameworks," emphatically making this emboldened claim: "However, AFs make the assumption that all attacks between arguments are certain (i.e., present attacks are known to exist, and missing attacks are known to not exist), which can in various settings be a restrictive assumption. A generalization of AFs to incomplete AFs was recently proposed as a formalism that allows the representation of both uncertain attacks and uncertain arguments in AFs. In this article, we explore the impact of allowing for modeling such uncertainties in AFs on the computational complexity of natural generalizations of acceptance problems to incomplete AFs under various central AF semantics" (article co-authored by Dorothe Baumeister, Matti Järvisalo, Daniel Neugebauer, Andreas Niskanen, and Jörg Rothe).

Here's what that means.

During the crafting of a legal argument, you might at some portions of your argument not have any idea of what type of counterarguments are going to be used against you. Thus, you have a kind of gap or hole in your own argument because you can't conjure up any potential counterargument to the particular arguing point.

Your argument is said to be incomplete.

In addition, you might come up with some counterarguments but they seem weak to you and loosey-goosey. As such, you might rate those as uncertain. You are uncertain in various ways. For example, perhaps you are uncertain as to whether the postulated counterarguments make any viable sense, or you are uncertain as to whether the opposing side would even employ such ostensibly flimsy counterarguments, etc.

Your argument is said to contain uncertainties.

The reality of practicing law is that you are inevitably and inexorably going to have legal arguments that are at times incomplete and also are bound to contain uncertainties. That's the bad news. The good news is that progress in the realm of AI computational argumentation is being made toward incorporating the incompleteness and infusion of uncertainty that already permeates day-to-day lawyering arguments.

Conclusion

To this end, we are boosting AI computational argumentation toward being a more relevant and practical tool for attorneys.

If you ascribe too to the notion that we will one day eventually have AI-based legal reasoning systems that are on par with human lawyers, the embodiment of incompleteness and uncertainty would seem to be a proper step in that direction.

Had Sun Tzu been a lawyer, perhaps he would have said that you ought to know thy argument and know the argument of thy opposition.

Someday, AI might be doing that for you.

.

Note: *For supplemental materials depicting the aspects discussed in this chapter, refer to Appendix B, which contains various augmented diagrams, charts, and additional related facets of relevance.*

CHAPTER 17

AI & LAW: WINOGRAD SCHEMA CHALLENGE

Key briefing points about this essay:

- Words matter, especially in the field of law
- A recent case was appealed due to the meaning differences of "typically" versus "normally"
- Some see daylight between those two words, others assert they are synonyms
- AI systems that use natural language capabilities are faced with similar issues
- The Winograd Schema Challenge in the AI field showcases these difficulties

Introduction

Lawyers seem to relish the thought-provoking aspects of solving word puzzles.

In a moment, I'll be asking you to ponder the meaning of something that is *typically* occurring versus something that is *normally* occurring. You'll see that this is ostensibly a challenging legal matter. Make sure to put your legal beagle thinking cap on.

First, some foundational aspects to set the scene appropriately.

Lawyers and judges are attentive to the meaning of words. This makes indubitable sense since our laws are based on words. We need to mindfully divine what those words purport to suggest in a myriad of real-world contexts.

A recent ruling by the 9th U.S. Circuit Court of Appeals provides a fascinating look at the nature of word meaning and perhaps word-splitting too. In short (leaving out numerous details for sake of discussion herein), there was a quite intriguing case involving a dispute concerning the differences if any between the word "typically" versus the word "normally" (in Innova v. Baran, No. 19-16849).

For this particular case, the U.S. District Court for the Northern District of California had essentially ascertained that there was a sufficiently significant difference between those two words. As we are apt to say in the legal profession, there is seemingly notable daylight between the word "typically" and the word "normally" such that they are distinctive of each other.

The plaintiff-appellant believed that the ruling was erroneous, namely that there is no worthy difference between those two words, and thusly appealed the case.

What do you think?

Weigh carefully in your mind whether you would contend that "typically" and "normally" are equal and synonymous, or whether they are demonstratively distinct and differentiable. Please cast your vote now. Don't continue reading this discussion until you've made your Gordian knot choice.

Okay, now that you've staked your career and reputation on which way you've chosen (sorry, just kidding), this is what the 9th Circuit Court opinion says: "While it is theoretically possible that there is 'space' between normally, most, and typically, that space is at best molecular, and nowhere big enough for the doublespeak freight train that USCIS tries to drive through it" (note that USCIS is the United States Citizenship and Immigration Services, which is the defendant-appellee and had as designated contact Kathy Baran as Director of the California Service Center).

Per the 9th Circuit Court, this is an open and shut matter, stating succinctly and without reservation that 'typically' and 'normally' are synonyms. Lest you think they are alone in that sentiment, they opted to bolster their position by making this bolstering assertion: "The Supreme Court uses these words interchangeably in the same sentence. So do we. So does the United States Solicitor General. And so does the federal government."

One supposes you could argue that the wisdom of the crowd is ergo ample proof for this ironclad-like finding that those two words are utter synonyms of each other. Of course, we ought to not hold our breaths on that presumption. You can bet your bottom dollar that there will inevitably be a case that somehow does manage to squeeze daylight between the two words and makes it stick.

I bring up this conundrum about word meanings to highlight some remarkably salient aspects of AI.

You see, the advent of AI in the law is perhaps harder than you think it is going to be, partially due to the slipperiness and deftness of words and their meanings. Trying to craft AI-based legal reasoning systems that use Natural Language Processing (NLP) akin to Alexa or Siri is more problematic than meets the eye, as it were.

AI Natural Language Challenges

Consider a famous ongoing challenge or contest in the field of AI that has to do with being able to analyze and interpret our natural language utterances. I'm referring to the Winograd Schema Challenge (WSC) that has been bandied around since about 2012.

This all began by a well-known professor of computer science named Terry Winograd when he asked whether an AI system could resolve these two sentences:

(1) The city council refused the demonstrators a permit because they feared violence.

(2) The city council refused the demonstrators a permit because they advocated violence.

Try to do some thoughtful word parsing and determine what each sentence portends.

Note that both sentences are ambiguously phrased. The resolution to the meaning of the respective sentences hinges on how you opt to assign the pronoun of "they" in the sentences. By and large, humans interpret the first sentence to be indicative that the city council feared violence, while the second sentence implies that the demonstrators are advocates of violence.

This seemed like a handy means of testing AI systems and their NLP, so much so that another computer scientist named Hector Levesque made this into an ongoing challenge. A database of specially prepared sentences reflecting these kinds of meaning-oriented ambiguities is available for use by anyone that wants to see how good their AI is.

Humans resolve these sentences to a consistency level of over 90% of the time, while the latest WSC contest in 2019 that tested numerous submitted AI systems topped out at 79.1% as the best that could be attained.

Worse still, some AI systems achieve their scores by somewhat cheating at this task. For example, suppose we had the sentence "The lions ate the zebras because they are predators" (this is covered in a handy research article in the *Communications of the ACM,* September 2021, discussing a newer version of the WSC coined as the WinoGrande).

We are all likely to interpret the "they" as referring to lions since we know that lions are predators of zebras. I assume you did likewise.

Some of the cheating-like AI systems skip past the lion-zebra relationship and instead statistically rely on the aspect that the word "lion" and the word "predator" are highly correlated. In that sense, it makes no difference what word was in the middle of the sentence. If I changed the sentence and said "The lions ate the crocodiles because they are predators" this would make things murkier for us humans since we also associate crocodiles as being predators too, but the skewed AI would still cling to the easy choice of lions due to that statistical bonding of lions-as-predators.

Bringing this back to the legal realm, I began this discussion by pointing out that humans can get into heated debates and heartily disagree about whether the word "typically" is the same as or different from the word "normally" (rising indeed to the appeals courts). This type of semantic ambiguity is a thorn in the side of human lawyers and human jurists.

Conclusion

AI is not going to magically make those legal word-splitting dilemmas disappear. The tough nut to crack of getting AI to embody legal reasoning on par with humans is going to arise in the muddy waters of semantic ambiguity exemplifying natural language.

I might say that this is *typically* or *normally* going to be the case, but I'll go out on a limb and decry that semantic ambiguity is *always* going to persist.

.

Note: *For supplemental materials depicting the aspects discussed in this chapter, refer to Appendix B, which contains various augmented diagrams, charts, and additional related facets of relevance.*

CHAPTER 18

AI & LAW: LEGAL VOLITION

Key briefing points about this essay:

- Volition is considered the legal core grounding of willful acts
- Mens rea sits atop volition and serves as an instantiation of a guilty mind
- We generally accept those precepts regarding humans and agency
- The question being battled is whether AI is in the same bailiwick
- Some far off futuristic AI might be, but not the AI of today

Introduction

Volition is a somewhat nebulous notion and has consumed rapt attention by philosophers, neuroscientists, and of course lawyers too. As you likely know, volition is loosely defined as acting with a semblance of mindful will.

This is considered in stark contrast to an act that might be involuntarily undertaken or one that occurs via some autonomic reflex. The thing is, not everyone entirely agrees to that kind of distinction, and ergo there is a lot of murkiness about what volition truly consists of.

When you spontaneously withdraw your hand from atop a hot stove, is this an act of volition or is it not?

Some would vehemently argue it is most definitely not an exemplar of volition. There was no thinking involved on your part and your core instincts simply took over. Others though would readily contest that claimed depiction. They would compellingly argue that your mind was engaged to the degree that it detected the dire circumstance and commanded that your hand and arm should abruptly escape the potential harm.

Let's give due attention then to this handy definition of volition and torts from the LexRoll Law Encyclopedia: "To establish an intentional tort, the plaintiff must prove a wrongful volitional act, done by the defendant with the intent, which causes injury to the plaintiff. The wrongful act by the defendant must be volitional." Note the crucial point that an intentional tort has volition at its core.

We can add to this motley stew the notion of mens rea.

Per your legal training, mens rea is the Latin term for having a guilty mind, namely acting with criminal intent. It is easy to blur together volition and mens rea, as though they are two peas in the same pod. That would be a mistaken combobulation. They are not the same thing. Indeed, without volition, there can ostensibly be no mens rea. On the other hand, a lack of mens rea has no bearing on whether volition exists or not.

Volition is the rock bed. Mens rea can potentially be atop it, and for which mens rea can only arise if indeed volition prior exists.

Mens rea is forever associated with the legendary quote by Justice Holmes about what a dog knows, as frequently quoted in discussions delineating means rea, such as mentioned in this particular passage: "Establishing the mens rea of an offender is usually necessary to prove guilt in a criminal trial. The prosecution typically must prove beyond reasonable doubt that the defendant committed the offense with a culpable state of mind. Justice Holmes famously illustrated the concept of intent when he said "even a dog knows the difference between being stumbled over and being kicked."

The mens rea requirement is premised upon the idea that one must possess a guilty state of mind and be aware of his or her misconduct; however, a defendant need not know that their conduct is illegal to be guilty of a crime" (per the Cornell Law School, Legal Information Institute).

Why am I dragging you through these seemingly basic definitions that are part and parcel of law school 101 kinds of instruction?

Because of Artificial Intelligence (AI).

AI And The Unthinkable Legal Debate

One of the most fractious debates taking place these days entails whether we ought to hold AI responsible for wrongful acts. In short, some assert that a variant of legal personhood ought to be attributed to AI, while others insist that this is entirely ludicrous and exhort that AI deserves no such coronation.

Allow me a moment to soundly clarify that there isn't any AI as yet that is sentient. Furthermore, despite whatever the news media might proclaim in brazen headlines, we are not anywhere close to having AI that achieves sentience. AI and sentience are not in the same ballpark.

I'm not suggesting this phenomenon will never happen, so don't jump that far, but I do want to abundantly make clear that we don't know at what far point in the future this might happen, nor can anyone say with certainty that the vaunted moment will occur at all.

Do not hold your breath for it.

Okay, so we hopefully agree that there is no sentient AI and we find ourselves within the midst herein of discussing volition and mens rea. They all tie together in an essential manner.

Take a moment to reflect on this insightful commentary in the *University of Pennsylvania Law Review* by legal scholar Robert Audi: "We might say, in line with both philosophical tradition and common speech, that volitions are acts of will; but no plausible volitional theory-which I shall call "volitionalism" for short-posits a substantive will as a kind of agent capable of its own acts. If volitions are acts of any kind, as opposed to events that underlie acts, they are acts of an agent in the ordinary sense of the term "agent" as applicable to persons."

The crux of the legal matter is whether or not AI can be labeled as an "agent" in an analogous way that we would characterize human beings as having agency. The seeming logic is that agents (of any kind) are volitional and per this volitionalism we can then hold them legally responsible for their acts.

Humans are generally viewed as agents and able to carry out volitional acts. That is pretty much a given. If you are willing to toss AI into the agency rubric, AI too would presumably imbue legal responsibility.

A fascinating legal research paper entitled "Criminal Liability of Autonomous Agents: From The Unthinkable To The Plausible" and authored by Pedro Miguel Freitas, Francisco Andrade, and Paulo Novais aspires to address these mind-bending considerations. For AI as we know of it today, the researchers persuasively argue that it is a mighty uphill battle to legally pin the tail on the donkey that AI showcases any iota of volition.

Per their remarks: "This fact makes clear that AI entities should only be made criminally accountable if they voluntarily acted, which means that must be an act done with will, volition or control. Accordingly, we cannot say that an AI entity voluntarily acted if the presence of one of these internal elements, depending on what particular theory one follows on the characterization of the "voluntarily" concept, is not found in a certain situation. While these elements describe a certain internal state of the agent, they should not however be confused with mens rea. There can be volition without mens rea, but the contrary is not true."

Conclusion

It is a bridge too far for those that are overstretching legal entities to encompass contemporary AI. The research paper alludes to a future such possibility, but urges that we not jump the gun, as it were: "While we may find easy to note that volition and human acts generally appear hand in hand, and so in the acts of legal entities, to plunge into the same conclusion as to AI entities' acts would arguably be precipitated."

You are welcome to think about AI that might someday embody volition and possibly have a dollop of mens rea. Be forewarned that some legal scholars curtly contend that all of this is imminently unthinkable.

I'm not one that usually goes along with the never say never mantra.

.

Note: *For supplemental materials depicting the aspects discussed in this chapter, refer to Appendix B, which contains various augmented diagrams, charts, and additional related facets of relevance.*

CHAPTER 19

AI & LAW: SHADOW DOCKET

Key briefing points about this essay:

- The U.S. Supreme Court has increasingly been producing so-called shadow decisions
- These are legal cases that were placed onto a shadow docket of SCOTUS
- Angst arises that the shadow case rulings are terse and without any judicial explanation
- This is said to be done for sake of expediency, though some say this is being outstretched
- AI-based legal reasoning systems are expected to be fast, so will they be shadowy too?

Introduction

You are likely aware of a famous radio show that arose in the 1930s that was called the *Detective Story Hour*. Just in case that doesn't ring a familiar bell, I'm sure this will: *The Shadow knows!*

At the rapt conclusion of each episode for the popular radio show, the narrator made us aware that The Shadow is seemingly all-knowing and omniscient. What the rest of us don't know is altogether known by this mysterious character.

Yes, indeed, ominously the shadow knows.

Maybe so, but the problem is that the rest of us don't particularly know what the shadow knows, principally because the shadow isn't saying what it knows. That is the increasingly vocal complaint that many are exhorting about the U.S. Supreme Court and its ever-growing number of so-called shadow decisions.

As you likely know, SCOTUS maintains a shadow docket from which shadow rulings are being issued. The basis for referring to all of this as shadow work is that the resultant judicial decisions are typically quite terse and lacking in any of the normally carefully crafted and fully elicited explanations.

Whereas we conventionally consider the Supreme Court to be the pinnacle of legal argumentation and jurisprudential acumen, the shadow rulings are barren of oral arguments, bereft of lengthy written opinions, mysteriously unsigned, and absent of any viable legal reasoning. The decision is the decision, whether you like it or not. Trying to argue about the decision is ostensibly like doing shadow boxing. There isn't any there to be fought and no opportunity to discern what led the Justices to reach their weighty conclusion.

The moniker of being a shadow docket is attributed to Professor William Baude at the University of Chicago Law School per his article in the *New York University Journal of Law & Liberty* (January 2015), arising from a lament about the rising tide of terse and scantily justified rulings by SCOTUS: "In important cases, it granted stays and injunctions that were both debatable and mysterious. The Court has not explained their legal basis and it is not even clear to what extent individual Justices agree with those decisions." Baude then coins this phenomenon with the catchy label that subsequently became the prevailing lingo: "As the order list comes to new prominence, understanding the Court requires us to understand its non-merits work – its shadow docket."

You might be assuming that since the Supreme Court keeps leaning toward using the shadow docket that the Justices are undoubtedly enamored of it.

They can merely make proclamations and dispense with all of that otherwise tiresome justification and legal mumbo jumbo. Like a parent that is weary of having to explain to their children why the youngsters aren't being allowed to play in the kitchen, all that is apparently needed is a brazen and summarily curt royal command. Take my orders, SCOTUS roars and begone.

That leaves a rather poor taste in the mouths of lawyers and jurists throughout the entire court system. A final decree from on top that proffers little or n logic is not very useful as a guiding light. The lower courts can't be sure what the legal meaning portends. A guessing game ensues and can cause the courts to ramble around with all kinds of speculation about what the legal ruling signifies.

Even some of the esteemed Supreme Court members have overtly expressed reservations about this shadow docket thing. Justice Kagan recently stated: "The majority's decision is emblematic of too much of this Court's shadow-docket decision-making — which every day becomes more unreasoned, inconsistent, and impossible to defend" (contained in the dissent of *Whole Woman's Health v. Jackson*, No. 21A24). In a similar vein, Justice Breyer said this in a recent interview published in the New York Times (August 27, 2021): "I can't say never decide a shadow-docket thing. Not never. But be careful. And I've said that in print. I'll probably say it more."

With all this seemingly untoward shading about the shadow docket, why is it being used and increasingly being relied upon?

Tradeoff Of Speed Versus Explanation

The claimed basis for the shadow approach is primarily to achieve speed.

Whereas the usual process of the Supreme Court takes gobs and gobs of time, those shadow decisions can be rendered at lightning-like speed. By skipping past the time required for collecting arguments, composing arguments, writing decisions, and the like, SCOTUS can move along at breathtaking speeds. Faster than a speeding bullet, at least in the context of making lofty legal decisions.

In that sense, you can readily be persuaded that sometimes a shadow ruling is entirely proper and expedient.

This takes us to a bruhaha that has been brewing in the realm of AI and the law. Some legal pundits are convinced that once we are able to attain AI-based legal reasoning systems, the AI will be able to produce legal rulings at unheard-of speeds. Press a button and the AI generates a legal decision in mere seconds, perhaps even in milliseconds or nanoseconds.

Does that imply that the use of AI-based legal reasoning systems is going to take us further and further down the rabbit hole of unexplained and unreasoned legal rulings?

Not necessarily.

If the AI is crafted with a sufficiently capable explanation facility, known as XAI for explainable AI, the odds are that we can have both speed and a fully aligned legally sound justification that goes with the rapidly derived judicial decision. It is a twofer.

On the other hand, some of today's AI systems are employing mathematically arcane aspects of Machine Learning and Deep Learning, for which there is no easy path toward producing a logically comprehensible result. By allowing those kinds of non-explainable approaches, we could easily end up in the same boat as the SCOTUS shadow docket. All that the AI would produce is a judicial decision and the underlying legal basis would be altogether murky and unrevealed.

It sure seems hard to imagine that we would paint ourselves into such a corner. Envision a legal world that is devoid of suitable transparency, has no discernable legal rigor, wields inexplicable judicial power, and sets precedents that are baffling to all.

Conclusion

Wait for a second, does that depict only an AI-based adjudication era or does it potentially predict the legal future if SCOTUS continues to brazenly expand upon the use of their shadow docket? That is a question of indubitable legal merit and needs some bright lights and sparkly sunshine to ascertain how much more shadowing we collectively believe is mindfully warranted.

A seemingly inarguable assertion is that the shadow knows, and so should everyone else.

Note: *For supplemental materials depicting the aspects discussed in this chapter, refer to Appendix B, which contains various augmented diagrams, charts, and additional related facets of relevance.*

CHAPTER 20
AI & LAW: LEGAL REDUCTIO

Key briefing points about this essay:

- One of the strongest tools a lawyer can exploit entails reductio ad absurdum
- Attacking an opponent's legal posture via reductio ad absurdum can be a big win
- You have to be careful and make sure that it holds up under scrutiny
- Plus ensure that your own legal arguments aren't susceptible either
- AI legal reasoning systems are gradually coming to your aid in this regard

Introduction

Reductio ad absurdum is immensely powerful.

Lawyers use it with great frequency. Judges use it abundantly too. When I say that those legal beagles make use of reductio ad absurdum, I wish to emphasize that there is a marked difference between appropriately using this sharp argumentation knife versus stabbing bluntly and ostensibly falsely.

First, let's start with the fundamentals.

It is perhaps blatantly obvious that reductio ad absurdum translates from the original Latin into everyday English as straightforwardly meaning "reduction to absurdity." You can try to crush your opponent's legal position by turning it into absurdist legal mush. This can be done by a step-by-step effort of logically reducing their argument into a series of illogical or contradictory conclusions.

A more holistic way to refer to this argumentation strategy is that it entails argumentum ad absurdum. Namely, in due course, you push the targeted argument into a ball of nearly laughable absurdity. Of course, when doing this kind of attack in a legal context the odds are that there is no laughing matter involved. The reductio is intended to produce serious results and showcase the lack of legal logic in the targeted argument. Another moniker for this legal wrangling is that you are employing apagogical arguments.

Let's consider the veritable classic version of reductio ad absurdum (often denoted as classic-RAA).

The most popular angle of classic-RAA consists of doing a proof by contradiction. You do this by taking whatever your legal opponent has asserted and start your trickery by raising your eyebrows and verbalizing with heavy cynicism that there is a gaping contradiction in their legal posture.

We can use a mathematical example to simply illustrate this proof by contradiction and then shift it into notable legal examples. Your opponent states confidently that there is a largest number that ideally exists, for which there is no larger number. Upon clearing your throat, you loudly utter this is quite ridiculous fodder and you can dash it to smithereens.

Here's how. You indicate that let's pretend for sake of discussion that there is this claimed largest number. If we add the value of 1 to this so-called largest number, we indubitably have a number that is one greater than the claimed largest number. But this newly hatched greater number is obviously more than the originally argued largest number, which means it is no longer the largest number.

The premise that there was a largest number is shown to be false as based on a contradictory showing. You can refer to this as self-refuting, self-inconsistent, or my favorite is to smear my opponent by exploiting the juicy labeling that their work is self-annihilating.

For those of you that are fans of *The Big Bang Theory* television series, you might vaguely (or fondly) remember this dialogue in an episode entitled "The Dumpling Paradox" (airing initially in 2007):

Leonard: "Penny, if you promise not to chew the flesh off our bones while we sleep, you can stay."

Penny: "What?"

Sheldon: "He's engaging in reductio ad absurdum. It's the logical fallacy of extending someone's argument to ridiculous proportions and then criticizing the result. And I do not appreciate it."

I bring this up because another variant of reductio ad absurdum involves using a slippery slope method of destroying a legal argument, rather than always and exclusively using contradictions as your argumentation dagger. In the slippery slope, you try to showcase that whatever the position consists of can be shoveled along and will ultimately produce an absurd or presumably wholly impractical result.

There is also RAA that is considered strong versus weak. A strong reductio has all the bases covered. A weak reductio is flimsy and subject to attack.

Consider how legal scholar Michael Shapiro uses the sword of reductio ad absurdum to ostensibly cut into the position of Chief Justice Burger in the U.S. Supreme Court case of Clark v. Community for Creative Non-Violence (CCNV), 468 US 288 (1984).

You get to be the judge of whether this is strong RAA or weak RAA.

First, some brief background.

The SCOTUS case dealt with unhoused or homeless that CCNV argued should be able to sleep in tents in a national park, per Shaprio's explanation: "The National Park Service, however, applied a no-camping regulation to the plan, which was to set up an array of symbolic tent cities for which a permit had been already issued. The CCNV and some individuals sued to prevent the no-camping regulation from being invoked against sleeping in the tents. The District Court issued a summary judgment for the Park Service, but the Eleventh Circuit reversed. In the end, the Supreme Court reversed, holding for the Park Service" (as covered in Shapiro's article "Argument Selection In Constitutional Law: Choosing and Reconstructing Conceptual Systems," Review of Law and Social Justice, 2009).

Shapiro then cuts to the chase, as it were: "Chief Justice Burger, concurring, presented a reductio ad absurdum argument against accepting the claim that sleeping in the park, if carried out as planned, would be a form of communication within the First Amendment's ambit. If one were to accept that argument, where would one stop? One would be logically committed to (at least briefly) insulating killings stipulated to be communicative. And even without going as far as claiming that homicide may be speech, it nonetheless "trivializes the First Amendment to seek to use it as a shield in the manner asserted here," by touting the park sleep-in as speech."

That's a smattering of reductio in action.

Adding AI Into The Mix

Shifting gears, we can bring AI into the picture.

AI is increasingly being used to aid lawyers and jurists in undertaking legal reasoning. There is an expectation that someday we will have fully capable AI legal reasoning systems that can perform on par with legal professionals.

Efforts are underway to craft AI that can identify legal arguments potentially susceptible to being undercut by reductio ad absurdum. The AI would point out the inherent absurdity or contradiction.

That is a decidedly handy tool for when analyzing an opponent's legal arguments.

Likewise, you could use that same AI-based capability to examine your own legal arguments. This is a prudent course of action. You would be better off to find your own possibly reductio foibles rather than letting an opponent or a doubting judge find it for you.

Conclusion

Be aware though that getting AI to accomplish this kind of legally astute analysis is not especially easy. Some sarcastically say they will believe it when they see it. Indeed, such pessimists proclaim that if it is true that AI can do this then pigs can fly. Since we seemingly know that pigs can't fly, this is a sneakily lobbed reductio at the AI postulate.

On the other hand, another handy reductio is one of my favorite all-time lines.

Note: *For supplemental materials depicting the aspects discussed in this chapter, refer to Appendix B, which contains various augmented diagrams, charts, and additional related facets of relevance.*

CHAPTER 21
AI & LAW: NON-CONTRADICATIONS RESOLUTE

Key briefing points about this essay:

- Lawyers are trained to ferret out legal contradictions
- Viewed another way, the assumption is that things are to be non-contradictory
- We all seem to be abide by the law of non-contradictions
- There are lots of nuances in the line between contradictions and non-contradictions
- AI legal reasoning systems are being developed to help in these matters

Introduction

You daily are likely watching for contradictions.

When you are closely inspecting a legal submission by opposing counsel, you are earnestly seeking to find contradictions that might undermine their side of the case. Similarly, when trying to aid your client that has seemingly transgressed a law or regulation, you might hope to spy a contradictory element in the law that could be the winning angle for your legal beagle efforts.

Rather though than focusing exclusively on contradictions, we can turn the matter somewhat upside down and consider the need for *non-contradictions*.

Say what?

Yes, the proverbial yin and the yang of contradictions is that you are customarily assuming that everything will be non-contradictory. You might examine some legal text and find an aspect that sticks out as contradictory. This implies that all the rest of the material was presumably non-contradictory.

We abide by the *law of non-contradiction*.

Of course, the so-called LNC or law of non-contradiction is not particularly a traditional "law" per se, at least not in the sense of a judicially divined or legislatively derived law. It is instead a philosophical construct. Some would prefer that the whole matter be relabeled as the PNC or the principle of non-contradiction, which might then reduce any confusion between being construed as a veritable *law of the land* versus a kind of natural law regarding human language and mathematical logic.

Simply stated, non-contradiction means that two things that are specified as strident opposites cannot be considered true at the same time. A light switch is either on or off. If you proclaimed that the light switch was simultaneously both on and off, this would seem to be a contradiction. For those aspects in life that we assert are mutually exclusive, a designated instance of two polar states cannot coexist concurrently and any claim thereof is considered contradictory.

We keep order and stability in our minds by adhering to the principle or law of non-contradiction. If you come across a situation of apparent contradiction, you are apt to immediately complain and insist that something has gone terribly awry. You want to turn the matter into a proper semblance of non-contradiction. This happens almost instinctively.

Aristotle is often credited as one of the earliest notable thinkers to delve into the nuances of non-contradiction. He long ago succinctly stated the matter for us: "It is impossible that the same thing belong and not belong to the same thing at the same time and in the same respect."

That being said, there are those today in the field of quantum physics and quantum mechanics that might grumble or outright disagree with this alleged need for non-contradiction (i.e., a particle is said to be in multi-states at the same moment in time and in the same physical space). For those of you that really like to think outside the box, you might want to consider reading up on the now-classic paradox of Schrödinger's cat.

You see, physicist Erwin Schrödinger played a kind of game or thought experiment with Albert Einstein in which a hypothetical cat is both alive and deceased at the same time (all part of the eeriness of the various quantum theories).

Setting aside the outlier notion of acceptance for straight-out contradictions, we can rest assured that by and large the world we live in is supposed to be non-contradictory. This is abundantly so in the practice of law.

Per the legal scholar Ricardo Alberto Caracciolo in his cornerstone 1979 article that appeared in *Philosophy of Law and Social Philosophy*, he points out: "The requirement that law, understood as a system of norms, has to be consistent, that is to say, it must lack contradictions, seems to be even stronger than the requisite of completeness." To make sure his meaning is abundantly clear, he goes on to emphasize: "The reasons for this postulate are easy to understand; a system can be qualified as inconsistent when two contradicting norms may demonstrate their validity within it."

In brief, if two laws are at opposite ends of each other, we abhor their joint existence if they are predicated on the same exact precepts and conditions. How can anyone hope to abide by a law that is entirely contradictory to itself? You are darned if you do and darned if you don't.

This is quite untenable situation and it taints the totality of law by being the bad apple in the barrel.

As an aside, there is also a haunting problem that any contradictory coexisting laws could ostensibly fall into the legal peril of *ex falso quodlibet* (Latin phrasing for the principle of logical explosion). Generally, this alludes to the notion that an allowed contradiction can be used to infer other falsehoods and generate a rather ugly series of deductively proper yet improper conclusions. That's not good.

AI Comes To The Rescue

Shifting gears, we can consider how AI might come to our aid on this non-contradiction pursuit.

AI is increasingly being used to aid lawyers and jurists in undertaking legal reasoning. There is an expectation that someday we will have fully capable AI legal reasoning systems that can perform on par with legal professionals.

Efforts are underway to craft AI that can analyze existing or proposed laws and try to ferret out potential pitfalls and guffaws. This could include detecting those perhaps thorny and maybe somewhat hidden contradictions.

You might be tempted to assume that humans on their own should readily be able to spot contradictions in our laws. Well, maybe not, or at least not in circumstances of voluminous laws and regulations.

For example, tax law expert John Prebble identifies some intriguing contradictions in the overwhelming morass of our existing tax laws (as examined in his paper entitled "Kelsen, the Principle of Exclusion of Contradictions, and General Anti-Avoidance Rules in Tax Law," published as a chapter in *Philosophical Foundations of Tax Law,* 2017).

He discusses at length one especially confounding example, describing a beguiling tax case regarding income spreading that the taxpayer asserted showcases contradictory properties: "The claim seems unmeritorious on its face. But the taxpayer has at least a semblance of a grievance if on one hand the statute allows him to spread his income for tax purposes and on the other hand denies him that right. The contradiction may not be a true contradiction in philosophical terms, but taxpayers can be forgiven for thinking that it is a kind of a contradiction that merits study."

It is assuredly not a contradiction to proffer that humans and AI can simultaneously be eyeing our laws for troublesome contradictions. This kind of searching and detection is actually harder than you might think.

Conclusion

Furthermore, a seeming contradiction can at times find a loosey-goosey way to wiggle out of the contradictory labeling and be interpreted as non-contradictory. One supposes that is assuredly what a good lawyer would try if their client depended upon the law being preferably viewed as non-contradictory.

You see, lawyers can at times be both contradictory and non-contradictory, seemingly in the same breath and at the same time (akin perhaps to Schrödinger's infamous theoretical cat.

Note: *For supplemental materials depicting the aspects discussed in this chapter, refer to Appendix B, which contains various augmented diagrams, charts, and additional related facets of relevance.*

CHAPTER 22
AI & LAW: SLIPPERY LEGAL SLOPES

Key briefing points about this article:

- We all talk about slippery slopes and routinely invoke this powerful metaphor
- This is especially true when discussing our laws and regulations
- Lawyers are apt to deal with alleged slippery slopes in the daily practice of law
- Slippery slopes are a dual-edged sword
- AI legal reasoning systems enter into the slippery slope conundrum too

Introduction

I'd be making a nearly sure bet that you are well-accustomed to the notion of a slippery slope. This is pervasive in our culture and seeming a ubiquitous concept and real-world matter.

It is certainly an oft-heard refrain when a new law is being proposed.

Those that oppose the formulating law are apt to quickly denounce the draft law as taking us down a sour and altogether bleak-ending slippery slope.

The law as currently composed might seem acceptable on the innocent face of it, but you are mindfully being forewarned that passage will inexorably lead to more and more such laws that are going to be throat choking, increasingly restrictive, and woefully dire.

Whether there is truly a slippery slope on the horizon is not necessarily a requirement for invoking the slippery slope metaphor. You can use the slippery slope in just about any circumstance, whenever you so please. If there is something that is about to get started that you immensely dislike, slam it fiercely with the slippery slope doomsday-based labeling.

Of course, slippery slopes do actually exist and there is certainly a rational basis to employ the slippery slope angst to try and forestall an adverse opening of the floodgates, as it were.

James Madison famously proffered this wisdom about slippery slopes when it came to our liberties: "It is proper to take alarm at the first experiment on our liberties. The freemen of America did not wait till usurped power had strengthened itself by exercise and entangled the question in precedents. They saw all the consequences in the principle, and they avoided the consequences by denying the principle" (as indicated in *Remonstrance Against Religious Assessments*, 1785).

I'm sure that you've experienced the slippery slope phenomenon in your law practice.

You might have been putting together a strident legal argument for a complex case and found yourself arguing that if your position does not prevail then it will spark a slippery slope of catastrophic consequences. Likewise, upon your reviewing the legal position of opposing counsel, you might assert that if they prevail then there will be a disastrous slippery slope that will ruin us all.

You see, slippery slopes can be quite handy. On the other hand, if someone is poking at you with a slippery slope legal argument, you have to try and defuse it and weaken the already presumed power that it intrinsically embodies.

Legal scholar Eugene Volokh has provided an excellent and enduring analysis of legal slippery slopes in his now-classic treatise entitled "The Mechanisms of Slippery Slope" as published in the 2003 edition of the *Harvard Law Review*. He defines a slippery slope in these straightforward terms: "I think the most useful definition of a slippery slope is one that covers all situations where decision A, which you might find appealing, ends up materially increasing the probability that others will bring about decision B, which you oppose."

I am always quick to think of the legendary fable of the camel's nose when I hear or read an invoking of a slippery slope. You might know it. The legendary tale is that a camel comes up to a tent in the desert and edges its nose into a small opening of the fabric. Gradually, the camel further inserts itself into the tent, until finally the entire camel is jampacked inside. As the aged proverb goes, beware of the camel's nose.

Returning to the legal analysis undertaken by Volokh, he points out that the already accepted standing of respecting legal precedents is yet another weighty keystone for slippery slopes within the legal domain: "One of the most common 'A will lead to B' arguments is the argument that judicial decision A would 'set a precedent' for decision B. This generally means that (1) A would rest on some justification J, and (2) justification J would also justify B."

One of the most readily employed attacks against a slippery slope tainted argument is that there is a falsehood underlying the axiomatic A-goes-to-B basis, as per the research article: "Each first step involves risk, but it is often a risk that we need to take. This need makes many people impatient with slippery slope arguments. The slippery slope argument, opponents suggest, is the claim that "we ought not to make a sound decision today, for fear of having to draw a sound distinction tomorrow."

All told, we would be wise to keep our eyes wide open for slippery slopes. If a situation exists that could entail a slippery slope, it might be worthwhile to explore the possibilities that this might portend. Rather than merely relying on gut instinct or a hunch, we would seem better off to mindfully and thoroughly contemplate all facets of the slippery slope, both good and bad.

Keep in mind too that a slippery slope can have positive connotations (it isn't inherently bad). There are times at which starting small is the only viable means to get underway. You might intend ergo to spur a slippery slope, perhaps doing so subtly and while under the radar. One supposes that if the end result is going to be beneficial and upright, even a hidden slippery slope could be considered acceptable.

There seems little doubt though that we commonly look at slippery slopes as presumably tending toward evil or something rather untoward, which is perhaps best expressed by the sage words of Aristotle: "The expense does not take place at once, and therefore is not observed; the mind is deceived, as in the fallacy which says that 'if each part is little, then the whole is little.' . . .In the first place, then, men should guard against the beginning of change."

AI On The Slippery Slope Bandwagon

Shifting gears, we can consider how AI might enter into the slippery slope conundrum.

AI is increasingly being used to aid lawyers and jurists in undertaking legal reasoning.

There is some mighty handwringing that if we let AI into the practice of law as an aid, this is going to be a darned awful slippery slope. The next thing you know, AI is doing the legal reasoning and human lawyers will no longer be needed. Start small, end big. Today's lawyers are going to be finding themselves out of a job, so say the slippery slope prognosticators.

A counterargument is that this kind of expansive AI is entirely fanciful and futuristic. If this ever happens, it will be many generations away in time. Meanwhile, we can leverage AI to do something quite useful for legal beagles.

We could use AI to ferret out slippery slopes in our laws, our proposed laws, and in the legal cases that are our your plate daily. In that sense, AI could assist in detecting the potentiality of legal-oriented slippery slopes, along with exhaustively expanding the underlying logic of what the slippery slope might ultimately produce.

Conclusion

A skeptic could acridly contend that you are letting AI proceed akin to allowing entry of the camel's nose. We are regrettably encouraging AI into the legal tent, they lament.

As wisdom tells us, be careful what you wish for.

Note: *For supplemental materials depicting the aspects discussed in this chapter, refer to Appendix B, which contains various augmented diagrams, charts, and additional related facets of relevance.*

CHAPTER 23

AI & LAW: UNINTENDED CONSEQUENCES

Key briefing points about this essay:

- We are seemingly all used to the possibility of unintended consequences
- Some conflate unintended with unanticipated, which is no longer in vogue
- There are intended versus unintended consequences of both good and bad
- Besides unintended consequences in the law, the same can be said of AI in the law
- A four-square indication of consequences about AI and the law is depicted

Introduction

Unintended consequences are the watchword of today's world. We are all aware nowadays that there is always seemingly a haunting possibility of unintended consequences. This is pretty much a given and few would be surprised at the notion that there are *both* intended and unintended consequences to our everyday actions and efforts.

No matter how carefully planned something might be, there is still a chance of those unintended consequences rearing their ugly head.

But wait for a second, perhaps we are being a bit hasty or cavalier by suggesting that unintended consequences must necessarily be bad. I dare say that there are times that unintended consequences can be okay, possibly even spectacularly so. Many well-known inventions and discoveries turned out to have enormously favorable consequences that went beyond the original inventor or discoverer in terms of their proffered initial intentions (e.g., penicillin, X-rays, Teflon, and so on).

Let's hark back to what is considered the earliest stake-in-the-ground about the nature of unintended consequences, namely a famous research article by Robert Merton of Harvard University in his 1936 landmark piece entitled "The Unanticipated Consequences of Purposive Social Action" (published in the American Sociological Review).

A quick clarification, he is sometimes improperly credited as the creator of the notion underlying unintended consequences, which even he makes clear is not the case, as per the very first line of his treatise that states this: "In some one of its numerous forms, the problem of unanticipated consequences of purposive action has been treated by virtually every substantial contributor to the long history of social thought."

One other important point that is worthy of noting is that Merton's article refers to *unanticipated* consequences, rather than using the word of referring to *unintended* consequences. For many years the academic literature and practitioners considered the words "unanticipated" and "unintended" to be entirely synonymous and retain identical meaning when it comes to labeling outcomes or consequences. Much of Merton's later work interchangeably uses those two words and so does nearly everyone else.

Gradually, this assumption has been usurped and altogether broken apart.

In 2015, Frank de Zwart at Leiden University emphasized that this persistent combobulation is an unfortunate conflation that needs to be righted: "The concept of unanticipated consequences, coined by Robert K. Merton (1936), has largely been replaced in current social science by its putative synonym, unintended consequences. This conflation suggests that unintended consequences are also unanticipated, effectively obscuring an interesting and real category of phenomena—consequences that are both unintended and anticipated— that warrant separate attention" (*Theory and Society*, "Unintended But Not Unanticipated Consequences").

Lawyers are of course sticklers about words and the meanings of words. Thus, I thought it useful to forewarn you that anyone seeking to conflate that which is construed as unintended with something that is ostensibly unanticipated does so on the rather loose ground these days.

The bona fide argument supporting their separate ways is based on the claimed fact that intention differs demonstratively from being able to imbue a capacity of foreseeability or anticipation. These are two decidedly different constructs, though forthrightly often related to each other. For more details underlying that particular argument, see a recent article "Play, Chat, Date, Learn, and Suffer? Merton's Law of Unintended Consequences and Digital Technology" by Mark Rosenbaum, Gabby Walters, Karen Edwards, Claudia Gonzalez, Germán Contreras Ramírez in *Academia Letters*, August 2021.

Anyway, we are absolutely on a firm footing that consequences can be either positive or negative in their impacts, or both, as explained by Merton: "Furthermore, unforeseen consequences should not be identified with consequences which are necessarily undesirable (from the standpoint of the actor). For though these results are unintended, they are not upon their occurrence always deemed axiologically negative."

Thinking In A Four-Square Chart

Laws are rife with unintended consequences.

The devisers of a new law might have the best of intentions and later realize that their crafted law produces the societal benefits desired and yet meanwhile also generates undesirable results. Astute attorneys are apt to recognize these negative outcomes before they even particularly materialize. A careful reading of a new law can sometimes showcase hidden adverse unintended consequences when scrutinized by a keen eye.

I've found that it is easiest to conceive of this overarching notion about intended versus unintended consequences as a set of four possibilities:

- Intended that produces beneficial consequences
- Intended that produces adverse consequences
- Unintended that produces beneficial consequences
- Unintended that produces adverse consequences

We can deftly apply this phenomenon to the advent of AI and the law.

First, be aware that AI is increasingly being used to aid lawyers and jurists in undertaking legal reasoning.

Some worry that AI-based legal reasoning might become so advanced that it works fully autonomously, being entirely on par with human attorneys and jurists. Does that envisioned future portend for positive consequences or negative consequences?

We can use our handy-dandy framework to explore this thorny question. Let's classify the future of AI and the law into the four buckets or categories, and in so doing we might have this set of interrelated but disparate consequences:

- Intended & beneficial – Justice for all will finally be attained by ready remote access to "robot" lawyers available 24x7 at pennies of today's costs.

- Intended & adverse – Human attorneys and jurists will be put out of work due to AI automation.

- Unintended & beneficial – Legal proceedings will be vastly accelerated, and the law will be openly leveraged beyond just those versed in the law as legal beagles per se.

- Unintended & adverse – Legal wrangling becomes epidemic and ubiquitous throughout society due to low barriers to entry and ease of touchscreen AI lawyering.

You might have some heartburn about those listed consequences, especially the aspect that human lawyers and judges might find themselves in the unemployment line. That possibility sure seems irksome and frightening when you've put all your stakes on becoming an attorney and having a long career practicing law.

The goods news for legal professionals is that the vaunted goal of AI that can sufficiently practice law on its own is nothing more than a dreamy fairytale right now. Sure, this might happen someday, far off in the distant future. It is a reasonable bet though that this won't arise during your generation.

Your law degree and legal career are pretty much assured, generally.

Conclusion

That being said, do not assume that you can rest on your laurels. You ought to anticipate that AI-augmented LegalTech is going to continue to arise and get better. Attorneys will find themselves being able to do more legal work at heightened quality levels, in lesser time, as a result of that AI-infused tech.

If you aren't keeping up with those AI supplemented tools, one might reasonably declare that the consequences for you and your legal practice could be adverse, perhaps intentionally or even unintentionally so.

Note: *For supplemental materials depicting the aspects discussed in this chapter, refer to Appendix B, which contains various augmented diagrams, charts, and additional related facets of relevance.*

CHAPTER 24
AI & LAW:
CREATIVE LEGAL THINKING

Key briefing points about this essay:

- Being considered a creative lawyer has both merits and drawbacks
- Part of the issue is that the word "creative" invokes a wide range of connotations
- Some fervently believe that the best lawyers are in fact creative lawyers
- How can lawyers all-told can be boosted in their creativity if they wish to do so?
- AI legal reasoning systems might be one handy tool for that creativity push

Introduction

Some welcome being referred to as a creative lawyer, while others might reject the moniker of being creative and prefer instead to be known as simply a steadfast lawyer. If we asked a roomful of attorneys to each raise their hand if any thought that they were particularly creative as a lawyer, what would happen?

I dare say that most would probably look around the room and first pointedly ask what does it mean to indicate that someone is a creative lawyer.

Given the predilection toward defining words and the need to be clear-cut about the meaning of words in the law, there would likely ensue a great clamor as the phrase "creative lawyer" was summarily picked apart.

Non-lawyers might immediately recoil at the notion of engaging a so-called *creative lawyer*. Heck, clients might exclaim, I just want a lawyer that will do their job. No need to be crazily creative. Just perform the required legal wrangling straightforwardly and somberly, doing whatever it is that lawyers seem to do.

In a now-classic analysis of creativity in the legal profession, Gordon MacLeod in his 1963 scholarly article entitled "Creative Problem Solving – For Lawyers?" in the *Journal of Legal Education* raised the question about whether attorneys ought to be creative or whether that is a bridge too far. His weighty conclusion was that of course creativity is desirable and even expected: "Perhaps the word 'creative' is a stumbling block. Creative means imaginative; and judgment, rather than imagination, is usually emphasized as the all-important attribute of a good lawyer. But it stands to reason that the lawyer who can use his imagination to come up with the greatest number of ideas for possible solutions is (after using his judgment to analyze the idea) most likely to come up with the best final answer to the problem."

The glaring problem with the word "creative" is that it conjures up a motley slew of attributes, ranging from highly desirable to wildly outcast and loathsome. Having a lawyer that can think outside the box and find innovative legal solutions is certainly prudent and likely preferred. But a presumably creative lawyer that goes overboard and tries outlandish legal skirmishes is not what clients are bound to want and nor would the legal profession all-told find especially endearing.

Even fellow attorneys and jurists are somewhat conflicted on the notion of creativity as a lawyer. MacLeod tried to ameliorate those concerns by stating it this way: "Many lawyers share the common misconception that creative problem-solving involves only imagination and thinking up new ideas. They are unaware that the systematic evaluation of ideas is a basic aspect of the creative problem-solving method. Judgment is not eliminated or even minimized; it is merely deferred to give the imagination a chance to operate."

Okay, so we might construe a creative lawyer as someone that can sensibly go beyond the norm, finding new ways and innovative avenues within the law, meanwhile not going bonkers and exceeding a semblance of general legal reverence that embodies a modicum of sanity in their capacity as an officer of the court.

Seasoned pros in the legal profession often worry that law schools seemingly knock creativity out of the heads of budding lawyers.

Legal scholars note the paradoxical elements of training to-be lawyers: "One notable conflict in the legal educational process is the paradox of creative analysis. While legal analysis often utilizes a considerable degree of creativity, it generally is framed by an overriding orthodoxy. This orthodoxy rewards technical proficiency and structural similarity over innovation and exploration" (per the article entitled "The Paradox of Creative Legal Analysis: Venturing Into The Wilderness" in the *University of Detroit, Mercy Law Review*, 2002).

Let's turn this topic on its head, as it were.

Assume that lawyers are by and large <u>not</u> creative and are ostensibly driven away from creativity, either by training or by personal tendencies on a pre-selection basis. In that case -- and I'm sure you'll find this disagreeable, we are perhaps faced with *half-brained lawyers* (not my words, that's what the research article "Comparative Legal Semiotics and the Divided Brain: Are We Producing Half-Brained Lawyers" posits in *The American Journal of Comparative Law*).

The article beseeches attorneys to wholeheartedly embrace creativity and without which such lawyers are missing the true art of practicing law: "Lus est art aequi et boni. These are the time-honored, opening words of the Roman Corpus Iuris (534 A.D.). They mean: Law is the art/craft (or craft/art) of the equitable and the good. Through the Corpus Juris is the basis of Western legal thinking (first filtered down and then promoted by the Catholic Church) this meeting of art and craft is largely forgotten – only the craft aspect persisted and took the upper hand: the lawyer as the craftsman."

How can we then prod attorneys toward the enlightenment of embracing creativity in the practice of law?

AI And The Creativity Inspiration

One means is arising via the advent of AI in the law.

You see, AI is increasingly being used to aid lawyers and jurists in undertaking legal reasoning.

Your initial gut reaction might be that AI is the complete opposite of creativity. AI would be good as a heads-down grind-it-out mechanism for doing e-Discovery or analyzing voluminous legal texts, but not somehow overreach into the human realm of being creative.

Admittedly, whether AI systems will exhibit creative capabilities is still an open question. Some argue that we can programmatically establish creativity in the various AI algorithms. Easy-peasy, they claim. Others are doubtful and counterargue that you are merely slapping the creativity label on something that is being unimaginatively routinized, absent of the spark of bona fide creative thinking.

Putting aside that rancorous debate, consider instead the notion of using AI to aid or spur human lawyers in a quest to embrace creativity. Maybe that's something we can agree is reasonably feasible.

A myriad of attempts at leveraging AI as a tool for instigating creative lawyering is indeed underway.

Initially, the approach involved using knowledge-based systems or expert systems. An example includes the work by Hajime Yoshino and Seiichiro Sakurai, as indicated in their paper "A Knowledge-Based Systems Approach to Educating Creative Legal Minds." They exhort that: "Good lawyers must have creative legal minds. It is important to educate law students so as to enhance creativity as well as to ensure their knowledge of the law. We have, therefore, established a project on the development of a legal education method for fostering creative legal minds."

More recently, other AI techniques and advanced technologies are being used.

For example, the Creative Profiler is devised to enhance the creativity of attorneys: "We introduce the Creative Profiler, as a comprehensive, state-of-the-art, assessment and training tool. Composed of research-validated tests of the most important dimensions of creative potential, the Creative Profiler is practical both for explaining the "multivariate" nature of creativity and mapping how it differs in different domains and professions, and also for helping individuals and groups develop creative talents in their chosen fields" (per the work by Todd Lubart and Branden Thornhill-Miller "Creativity in Law: Legal Professions and the Creative Profiler Approach" in *Mapping Legal Innovation*, 2021).

Conclusion

I'd readily bet that using AI to inspire creativity in human lawyers is well within the realm of the doable. That being said, will lawyers that eschew creativity be willing to arm themselves with such AI? It could be that only creative lawyers do so, in which case the need for such an AI tool seems somewhat muted.

Yet another paradox to be dealt with.

Note: *For supplemental materials depicting the aspects discussed in this chapter, refer to Appendix B, which contains various augmented diagrams, charts, and additional related facets of relevance.*

CHAPTER 25

AI & LAW: THINKING OUTSIDE THE LEGAL BOX

Key briefing points about this essay:

- People often find themselves mentally trapped inside a box, as it were
- Lawyers fall for this human foible too
- To clarify, sometimes its ok, while in other instances it is a drawback
- AI can be used as a tool to help lawyers think outside the box
- Efforts are underway to develop AI-based legal reasoning that can augment lawyers

Introduction

That darned box. It seems to be everywhere.

And you inevitably find yourself inside of it.

What am I talking about?

I'm alluding to the constant drumbeat that we all need to be thinking outside the box. You've undoubtedly been chided at some point for being confined in your thinking, ostensibly stuck inside a gloomy and overly constrained mental box.

The refrain about mindfully leaping beyond your blocked or confined thinking is nearly ubiquitous and used whether it applies or not.

To clarify, sometimes being wholly within the box is perfectly fine. A mere accusation that you are stinted in your thought processes due to some amorphous and perhaps illusory mind-limiting box is not an axiomatic cause to panic and believe you are wrong in your thinking.

In brief, you can be okay inside the box.

Likewise, you can be at times better off by getting outside the box. There are admittedly times that you are inside and surely ought to be outside, ergo having someone challenge you to remove your blinders and escape your own mental imprisonment can be quite beneficial.

On the other hand, there are equally times that veering beyond the box is a false proposition and you will waste time and energy in a fruitless and aimless pursuit. You need to thoughtfully realize whether you are potentially trapped inside a mental box, and then decide whether to go outside of it, and subsequently judge whether you were right, to begin with, and can satisfactorily settle back into the box.

Whew, that's an unsettling dollop of mental contortions.

To what end is this exhortation taking you?

It turns out that all of this applies to the legal realm and the act of practicing law.

There is a general assumption that attorneys are seemingly the box-going kind of thinkers. For example, one illustrative indication is that lawyers tend to specialize in specific areas of the law. Some lawyers are tax law experts, while some are criminal law attorneys, etc.

Those are boxes.

Even within a particular specialty, the assertion is that lawyers lean toward getting boxed in. They become so versed in the law of their chosen subfield that they know and seem to accept at face value the existing norms that have already been established. An attorney from outside the area of specialty might ask seemingly boneheaded legal questions, not realizing that they are treading on presumed solidified or sacrosanct legal ground.

Please be aware that this is not a diss against being inside a box. Boxes can be pretty handy. They provide a form of fencing that can be extremely useful. Once others get into that box with you, they often discover that their outsider perspective was naïve and mistaken.

Twisting this around, there is still that chance of finding something new or creative by easing yourself out of the box, or having a tool to help nudge you outside of the box.

In a moment, I'll proffer the notion that AI might be used for this kind of box-bursting impetus. Be aware that AI is increasingly being used to aid lawyers and jurists in undertaking legal reasoning.

AI And The Thinking Box

Let's start with an overall box-based topic and make our way to the AI possibilities.

Recent news coverage about a prominent legal matter showcases a prime example of thinking outside the box (note that the media is labeling the instance as an outside-the-box form of legal thinking) It turns out that legal scholar Jonathan Mitchell caused a bit of a stir due to the contemporary leveraging of his previously proclaimed writ-of-erasure fallacy.

I'll briefly lay out the surfaced fallacy.

Mitchell first identified a proclaimed legally confining box in his *Virginia Law Review* article of 2018: "The power of judicial review is all too often regarded as something akin to an executive veto. When a court declares a statute unconstitutional or enjoins its enforcement, the disapproved law is described as having been "struck down" or rendered "void" — as if the judiciary holds a veto-like power to cancel or revoke a duly enacted statute. And the political branches carry on as though the court's decision has erased the statute from the law books."

Mitchell then tells us why this is ostensibly a type of box in terms of our thinking about the matter: "But the federal judiciary has no authority to alter or annul a statute. The power of judicial review is more limited: It allows a court to decline to enforce a statute and to enjoin the executive from enforcing that statute. But the judicially disapproved statute continues to exist as law until it is repealed by the legislature that enacted it, even as it goes unenforced by the judiciary or the executive."

We now begin to see the shape of the box that he is pointing out to us all: "When judges or elected officials mistakenly assume that a court decision has canceled or revoked a duly enacted statute, they commit the "writ-of-erasure fallacy" — the fallacy that equates judicial review with a veto-like power to "strike down" legislation or delay its effective start date."

Thus, in recap, we might fall into the mental trap of assuming that simply because a court strikes down or renders void a duly enacted statute, the statute has been erased from the law. Not so fast, Mitchell notes. The law is still there. Presumably, in various creative ways, it can be potentially revived. One supposes it is akin to a zombie that might still get up from being knocked down. You don't know for sure that the darned thing is truly dead.

You would apparently be better off to think of said zombie statutes as temporarily in a non-enforcement mode. If you allow your mind to cross out the statute entirely as though it was wiped clean off this earth, you are inside a box that though most of the time is fine, there is a chance that you might miss other potential legal opportunities further down the pike.

Okay, with that example in hand, how might AI be of any use?

Those that are implementing AI for legal reasoning are apt to find fundamental assumptions that are otherwise taken for granted in our existent laws and legal practices. Thus, the pursuit of AI for use in the law is bound to unearth interesting boxes and shine a light on some outside-the-box possibilities.

In addition, those lawyers opting to leverage AI-based legal reasoning systems can have the AI challenge whatever laid out legal logic the attorney has predetermined. It is conceivable that the AI system will either spot a legal box or generate an outside-the-box inspiration.

Conclusion

We are not yet though anywhere near to devising AI that can engage per se in outside-the-box mental machinations. Right now, the AI is a nudge to humans, getting attorneys to realize when a box possibly exists and it might be useful to look beyond it.

Someday, we might end up with AI that can go outside the box on legal reasoning, for which human lawyers will either relish or potentially revile that kind of automation.

Note: *For supplemental materials depicting the aspects discussed in this chapter, refer to Appendix B, which contains various augmented diagrams, charts, and additional related facets of relevance.*

APPENDIX A
TEACHING WITH THIS MATERIAL AND BIBLIOGRAPHY

The essays in this book can readily be used as a reading supplemental to augment traditional textbook-oriented content, particularly used in a class on AI or a class about the law.

Courses where this material is most likely applicable encompass classes at a college or university level.

Here are some typical settings that might apply:

- Computer Science. Classes studying AI, or possibly a CS social impacts class, etc.

- Law. Law classes exploring technology and its adoption for legal uses.

- Sociology. Sociology classes on the adoption and advancement of technology.

Specialized classes at the undergraduate and graduate level can also make use of this material.

For each chapter, consider whether you think the chapter provides material relevant to your course topic.

There are plenty of opportunities to get the students thinking about the topics and encourage them to decide whether they agree or disagree with the points offered and positions taken.

I would also encourage you to have the students do additional research beyond the chapter material presented (I provide next some suggested assignments that they can do).

RESEARCH ASSIGNMENTS ON THESE TOPICS

Your students can find research and background material on these topics, doing so in various tech journals, law journals, and other related publications.

Here are some suggestions for homework or projects that you could assign to students:

a) Assignment for foundational AI research topics: Research and prepare a paper and a presentation on a specific aspect of AI, such as Machine Learning, ANN, etc. The paper should cite at least 3 reputable sources. Compare and contrast to what has been stated in the chosen chapter.

b) Assignment for Law topics: Research and prepare a paper covering Law aspects via at least 3 reputable sources and analyze the characterizations. Compare and contrast to what has been stated in the chosen chapter.

c) Assignment for a Business topic: Research and prepare a paper and a presentation on businesses and advanced technology regarding AI and Law. What is trending, and why? Make sure to cite at least 3 reputable sources. Compare and contrast to the depictions herein.

d) Assignment to do a Startup: Have the students prepare a paper or business plan about how they might start up a business in this realm. They could also be asked to present their business plan and should also have a prepared presentation deck to coincide with it.

You can certainly adjust the aforementioned assignments to fit your particular needs and class structure.

You'll notice that I usually suggest that (at least) 3 reputable cited sources be utilized for the paper writing-based assignments.

I usually steer students toward "reputable" publications, since otherwise, they will cite some less reliable sources that have little or no credentials, other than that they happened to appear online was easy to retrieve. You can, of course, define "reputable" in whatever way you prefer, for example, some faculty think Wikipedia is not reputable while others believe it is reputable and allow students to cite it.

The reason that I usually ask for at least 3 citations is that if the student only relies upon one or two citations, they usually settle on whatever they happened to find the fastest. By requiring 3 (or more) citations, it usually seems to inspire them to explore more extensively and likely end-up finding five or more sources, and then whittling it down to 3 if so needed.

I have not specified the length of their papers and leave that to you to tell the students what you prefer.

For each of those assignments, you could end up with a short one to two-pager or you could do a dissertation length in-depth paper. Base the length on whatever best fits for your class, and likewise the credit amount of the assignment within the context of the other grading metrics you'll be using for the class.

I usually try to get students to present their work, in addition to doing the writing. This is a helpful practice for what they will do in the business world. Most of the time, they will be required to prepare an analysis and present it. If you don't have the class time or inclination to have the students present their papers, then you can presumably omit the aspect of them putting together presentations.

GUIDE TO USING THE CHAPTERS

For each of the chapters, I provide the next some various ways to use the chapter contents.

You can assign the below tasks as individual homework assignments, or the tasks can be used for team projects. You can easily layout a series of assignments, such as indicating that the students are to do item "a" below for say Chapter 1, then "b" for the next chapter of the book, and so on.

a) What is the main point of the chapter and describe in your own words the significance of the topic.

b) Identify at least two aspects in the chapter that you agree with and support your concurrence by providing at least one other outside researched item as support; make sure to explain your basis for agreeing with the aspects.

c) Identify at least two aspects in the chapter that you disagree with and support your disagreement by providing at least one other outside researched item as support; make sure to explain your basis for disagreeing with the aspects.

d) Find an aspect that was not covered extensively in the chapter, doing so by conducting outside research, and then offer an expanded indication about how that aspect ties into the chapter, along with the added significance it brings to the topic.

e) Interview a specialist in the industry about the topic of the chapter, collect from them their thoughts and opinions, and readdress the chapter by citing your source and how they compared and contrasted to the material,

f) Interview a relevant professor or researcher in a college or university setting about the topic of the chapter, collect from them their thoughts and opinions, and readdress the chapter by citing your source and how they compared and contrasted to the material,

g) Try to update a chapter by finding out the latest on the topic and ascertain whether the issue or topic has now been solved or whether it is still being addressed, explain what you come up with.

The above are all ways in which you can get the students of your class involved in considering the material of a given chapter. You could mix things up by having one of those above assignments per each week, covering the chapters over the course of the semester or quarter.

SUGGESTED REFERENCES TO EXPLORE

To help get your students started in finding relevant and important papers on the topic of AI and the law, I provide next a handy bibliography that can be utilized.

You could also assign the students to each (or in teams) read an assigned reference from the list, and then have them provide either a written summary and review or do so as part of a classroom presentation.

BIBLIOGRAPHIC REFERENCES

1. Aleven, Vincent (1997). "Teaching Case-Based Argumentation Through a Model and Examples," Ph.D. Dissertation, University of Pittsburgh.

2. Aleven, Vincent (2003). "Using Background Knowledge in Case-Based Legal Reasoning: A Computational Model and an Intelligent Learning Environment," Artificial Intelligence.

3. Amgoud, Leila (2012). "Five Weaknesses of ASPIC+," Volume 299, Communications in Computer and Information Science (CCIS).

4. Antonious, Grigoris, and George Baryannis, Sotiris Batsakis, Guido Governatori, Livio Robaldo, Givoanni Siragusa, Ilias Tachmazidis (2018). "Legal Reasoning and Big Data: Opportunities and Challenges," August 2018, MIREL Workshop on Mining and Reasoning Legal Texts.

5. Ashley, Kevin (1991). "Reasoning with Cases and Hypotheticals in HYPO," Volume 34, International Journal of Man-Machine Studies.

6. Ashley, Kevin, and Karl Branting, Howard Margolis, and Cass Sunstein (2001). "Legal Reasoning and Artificial Intelligence: How Computers 'Think' Like Lawyers," Symposium: Legal Reasoning and Artificial Intelligence, University of Chicago Law School Roundtable.

7. Baker, Jamie (2018). "A Legal Research Odyssey: Artificial Intelligence as Disrupter," Law Library Journal.

8. Batsakis, Sotiris, and George Baryannis, Guido Governatori, Illias Tachmazidis, Grigoris Antoniou (2018). "Legal Representation and Reasoning in Practice: A Critical Comparison," Volume 313, Legal Knowledge and Information Systems.

9. Bench-Capon, Trevor (2004). "AGATHA: Automation of the Construction of Theories in Case Law Domains," January 2004, Legal Knowledge and Information Systems Jurix 2004, Amsterdam.

10. Bench-Capon, Trevor (2012). "Representing Popov v Hayashi with Dimensions and Factors," March 2012, Artificial Intelligence and Law.

11. Bench-Capon, Trevor, and Givoanni Sartor (2003). "A Model of Legal Reasoning with Cases Incorporating Theories and Values," November 2013, Artificial Intelligence.

12. Breuker, Joost (1996). "A Functional Ontology of Law," October 1996, ResearchGate.

13. Bruninghaus, Stefanie, and Kevin Ashley (2003). "Combining Case-Based and Model-Based Reasoning for Predicting the Outcome of Legal Cases," June 2003, ICCBR'03: Proceedings of the 5th International Conference on Case-based reasoning: Research and Development.

14. Buchanan, Bruce, and Thomas Headrick (1970). "Some Speculation about Artificial Intelligence and Legal Reasoning," Volume 23, Stanford Law Review.

15. Chagal-Feferkorn, Karni (2019). "Am I An Algorithm or a Product: When Products Liability Should Apply to Algorithmic Decision-Makers," Stanford Law & Policy Review.

16. Douglas, William (1948). "The Dissent: A Safeguard of Democracy," Volume 32, Journal of the American Judicature Society.

17. Dung, P, and R. Kowalski, F. Toni (2006). "Dialectic Proof Procedures for Assumption-Based Admissible Argumentation," Artificial Intelligence.

18. Eliot, Lance (2020). AI And Legal Reasoning Essentials. LBE Press Publishing.

19. Eliot, Lance (2020). Artificial Intelligence and LegalTech Essentials. LBE Press Publishing.

20. Eliot, Lance (2020). "FutureLaw 2020 Showcases How Tech is Transforming The Law, Including the Impacts of AI," April 16, 2020, Forbes.

21. Erdem, Esra, and Michael Gelfond, Nicola Leone (2016). "Applications of Answer Set Programming," AI Magazine.

22. Gardner, Anne (1987). Artificial Intelligence and Legal Reasoning. MIT Press.

23. Genesereth, Michael (2009). "Computational Law: The Cop in the Backseat," Stanford Center for Legal Informatics, Stanford University.

24. Ghosh, Mirna (2019). "Automation of Legal Reasoning and Decision Based on Ontologies," Normandie Universite.

25. Grabmair, Matthias (2017). "Predicting Trade Secret Case Outcomes using Argument Schemes and Learned Quantitative Value Effect Tradeoffs," IJCAI June 12, 2017, London, United Kingdom.

26. Hage, Jaap (1996). "A Theory of Legal Reasoning and a Logic to Match," Volume 4, Artificial Intelligence and Law.

27. Hage, Jaap (2000). "Dialectical Models in Artificial Intelligence and Law," Artificial Intelligence and Law.

28. Hage, Japp, and Ronald Leenes, Arno Lodder (1993). "Hard Cases: A Procedural Approach," Artificial Intelligence and Law.

29. Hobbes, Thomas (1651). The Matter, Form, and Power of a Common-Wealth Ecclesiasticall and Civil.

30. Holmes, Oliver (1897). "The Path of the Law," Volume 10, Harvard Law Review.

31. Katz, Daniel, and Michael Bommarito, Josh Blackman (2017). "A General Approach for Predicting the Behavior of the Supreme Court of the United States," April 12, 2017, PLOS ONE.

32. Kowalski, Robert, and Francesca Toni (1996). "Abstract Argumentation," AI-Law96.

33. Laswell, Harold (1955). "Current Studies of the Decision Process: Automation Creativity," Volume 8, Western Political Quarterly.

34. Libal, Tomer, and Alexander Steen (2019). "The NAI Suite: Drafting and Reasoning over Legal Texts," October 15, 2019, arXiv.

35. Lipton, Zachary (2017). "The Mythos of Model Interpretability," March 6, 2017, arXiv.

36. Martin, Andrew, and Kevin Quinn, Theodore Ruger, Pauline Kim (2004). "Competing Approaches to Predicting Supreme Court Decision Making," December 2014, Symposium on Forecasting U.S. Supreme Court Decisions.

37. McCarty, Thorne (1977). "Reflections on TAXMAN: An Experiment in Artificial Intelligence and Legal Reasoning," January 1977, Harvard Law Review.

38. Modgil, Sanjay, and Henry Prakken (2013). "The ASPIC+ Framework for Structured Argumentation: A Tutorial," December 16, 2013, Argument & Computation.

39. Mowbray, Andrew, and Philip Chung, Graham Greenleaf (2019). "Utilising AI in the Legal Assistance Sector," LegalAIIA Workshop, ICAIL, June 17, 2019, Montreal, Canada.

40. Parasuraman, Raja, and Thomas Sheridan, Christopher Wickens (2000). "A Model for Types and Levels of Human Interaction with Automation," May 2000, IEEE Transactions on Systems, Man, and Cybernetics.

41. Popple, James (1993). "SHYSTER: A Pragmatic Legal Expert System," Ph.D. Dissertation, Australian National University.

42. Prakken, Henry, and Giovanni Sartor (2015). "Law and Logic: A Review from an Argumentation Perspective," Volume 227, Artificial Intelligence.

43. Rissland, Edwina (1988). Artificial Intelligence and Legal Reasoning: A Discussion of the Field and Gardner's Book," Volume 9, AI Magazine.

44. Rissland, Edwina (1990). "Artificial Intelligence and Law: Stepping Stones to a Model of Legal Reasoning," Yale Law Journal.

45. Searle, John (1980). "Minds, Brains, and Programs," Volume 3, Behavioral and Brain Sciences.

46. Sunstein, Cass (2001). "Of Artificial Intelligence and Legal Reasoning," University of Chicago Law School, Public Law and Legal Theory Working Papers.

47. Sunstein, Cass, and Kevin Ashley, Karl Branting, Howard Margolis (2001). "Legal Reasoning and Artificial Intelligence: How Computers 'Think' Like Lawyers," Symposium: Legal Reasoning and Artificial Intelligence, University of Chicago Law School Roundtable.

48. Surden, Harry (2014). "Machine Learning and Law," Washington Law Review.

49. Surden, Harry (2019). "Artificial Intelligence and Law: An Overview," Summer 2019, Georgia State University Law Review.

50. Valente, Andre, and Joost Breuker (1996). "A Functional Ontology of Law," Artificial Intelligence and Law.

51. Waltl, Bernhard, and Roland Vogl (2018). "Explainable Artificial Intelligence: The New Frontier in Legal Informatics," February 2018, Jusletter IT 22, Stanford Center for Legal Informatics, Stanford University.

52. Wittgenstein, Ludwig (1953). Philosophical Investigations. Blackwell Publishing.

APPENDIX B
SUPPLEMENTAL FIGURES AND CHARTS

For the convenience of viewing, supplemental figures and charts related to the topics discussed are shown on the next pages

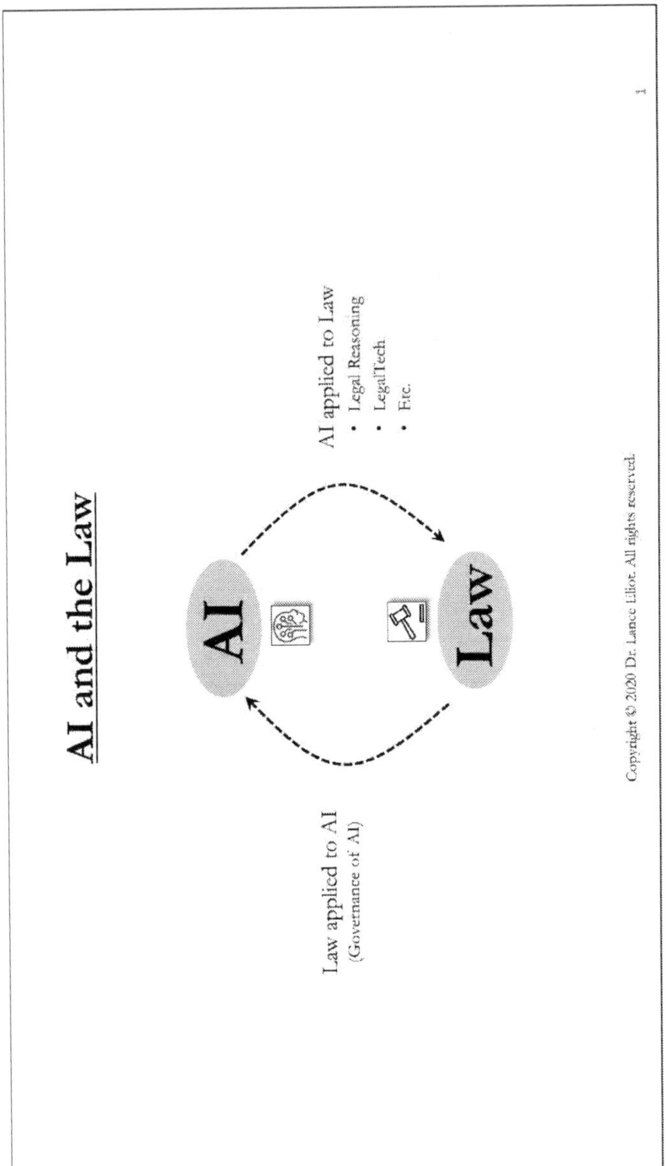
AI and the Law
AI
Law
AI applied to Law
• Legal Reasoning
• LegalTech
• Etc.
Law applied to AI
(Governance of AI)
Copyright © 2020 Dr. Lance Eliot. All rights reserved.
1

Figure 1

AI & Law: Levels of Autonomy For AI Legal Reasoning (AILR)

Level	Descriptor	Examples	Automation	Status
0	No Automation	Manual, paper-based (no automation)	None	De Facto - In Use
1	Simple Assistance Automation	Word Processing, XLS, online legal docs, etc.	Legal Assist	Widely In Use
2	Advanced Assistance Automation	Query-style NLP, ML for case prediction, etc.	Legal Assist	Some In Use
3	Semi-Autonomous Automation	KBS & ML/DL for legal reasoning & analysis, etc.	Legal Assist	Primarily Prototypes & Research Based
4	AILR Domain Autonomous	Versed only in a specific legal domain	Legal Advisor (law fluent)	None As Yet
5	AILR Fully Autonomous	Versatile within and across all legal domains	Legal Advisor (law fluent)	None As Yet
6	AILR Superhuman Autonomous	Exceeds human-based legal reasoning	Supra Legal Advisor	Indeterminate

Figure 1: AI & Law - Autonomous Levels by Rows

Source Author: Dr. Lance B. Eliot

V1.3

Figure 2

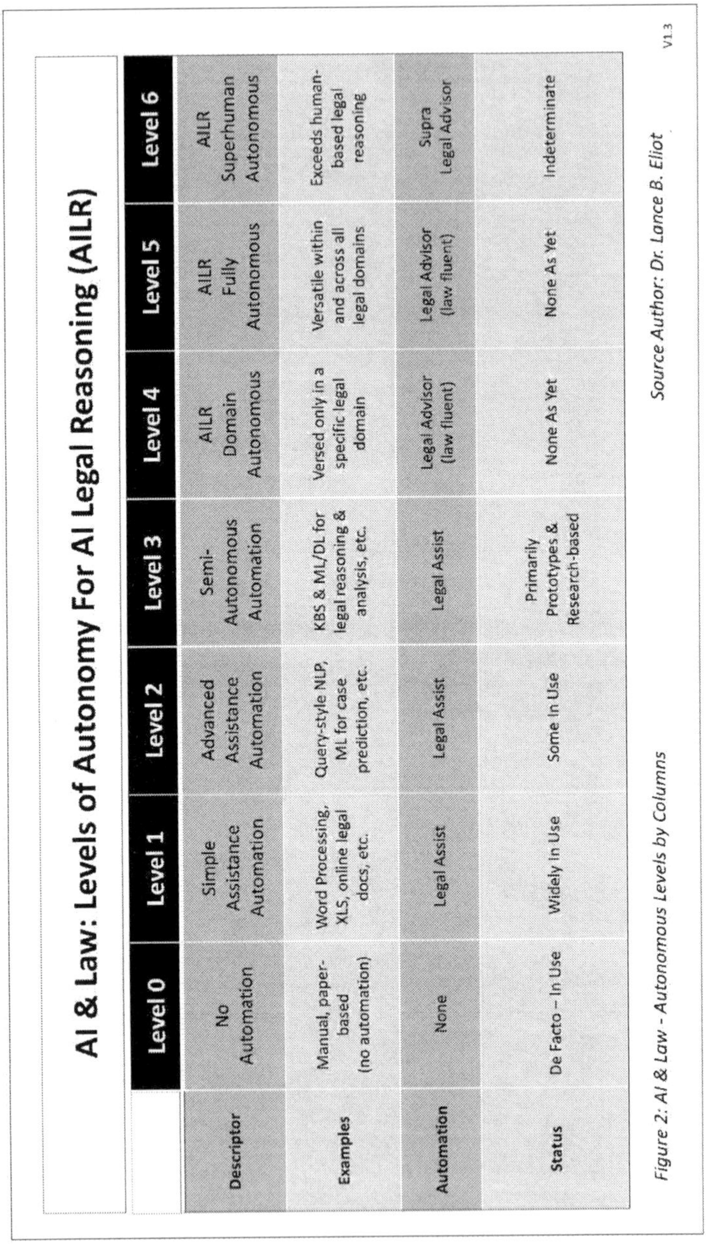

AI & Law: Levels of Autonomy For AI Legal Reasoning (AILR)

	Level 0	Level 1	Level 2	Level 3	Level 4	Level 5	Level 6
Descriptor	No Automation	Simple Assistance Automation	Advanced Assistance Automation	Semi-Autonomous Automation	AILR Domain Autonomous	AILR Fully Autonomous	AILR Superhuman Autonomous
Examples	Manual, paper-based (no automation)	Word Processing, XLS, online legal docs, etc.	Query-style NLP, ML for case prediction, etc.	KBS & ML/DL for legal reasoning & analysis, etc.	Versed only in a specific legal domain	Versatile within and across all legal domains	Exceeds human-based legal reasoning
Automation	None	Legal Assist	Legal Assist	Legal Assist	Legal Advisor (law fluent)	Legal Advisor (law fluent)	Supra Legal Advisor
Status	De Facto – In Use	Widely In Use	Some In Use	Primarily Prototypes & Research-based	None As Yet	None As Yet	Indeterminate

Figure 2: AI & Law - Autonomous Levels by Columns

Source Author: Dr. Lance B. Eliot

V1.3

Figure 3

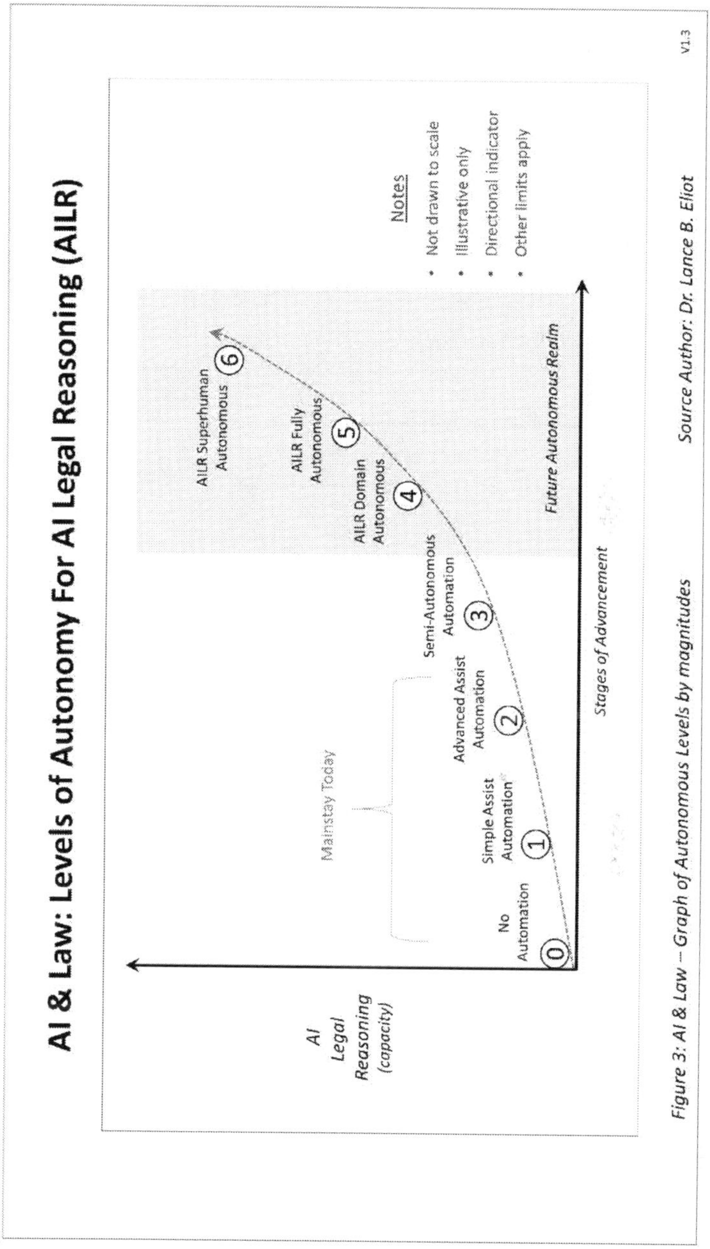

AI & Law: Levels of Autonomy For AI Legal Reasoning (AILR)
AI Legal Reasoning (capacity)
0 No Automation
1 Simple Assist Automation
2 Advanced Assist Automation
3 Semi-Autonomous Automation
4 AILR Domain Autonomous
5 AILR Fully Autonomous
6 AILR Superhuman Autonomous
Mainstay Today
Future Autonomous Realm
Stages of Advancement
Notes
Not drawn to scale
Illustrative only
Directional indicator
Other limits apply
Figure 3: AI & Law -- Graph of Autonomous Levels by magnitudes
Source Author: Dr. Lance B. Eliot
V1.3

Figure 4

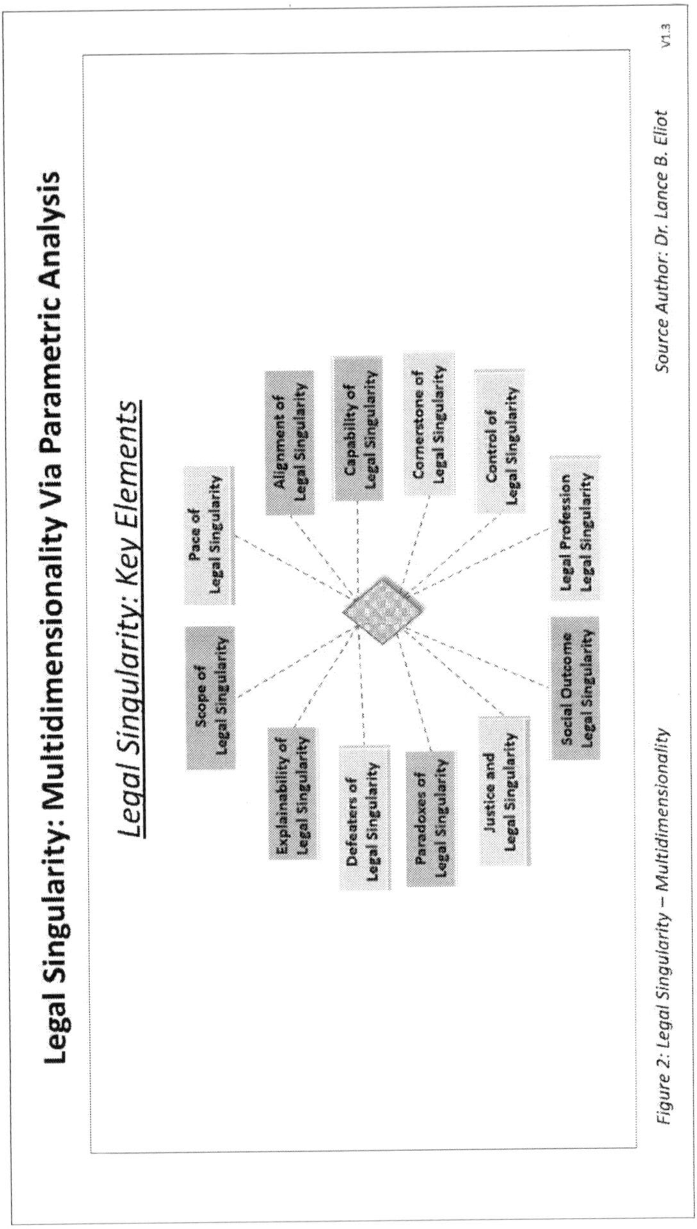
Legal Singularity: Multidimensionality Via Parametric Analysis
Legal Singularity: Key Elements
Pace of Legal Singularity
Alignment of Legal Singularity
Capability of Legal Singularity
Cornerstone of Legal Singularity
Control of Legal Singularity
Legal Profession Legal Singularity
Social Outcome Legal Singularity
Justice and Legal Singularity
Paradoxes of Legal Singularity
Defeaters of Legal Singularity
Explainability of Legal Singularity
Scope of Legal Singularity
Figure 2: Legal Singularity – Multidimensionality
Source Author: Dr. Lance B. Eliot
V1.3

Figure 5

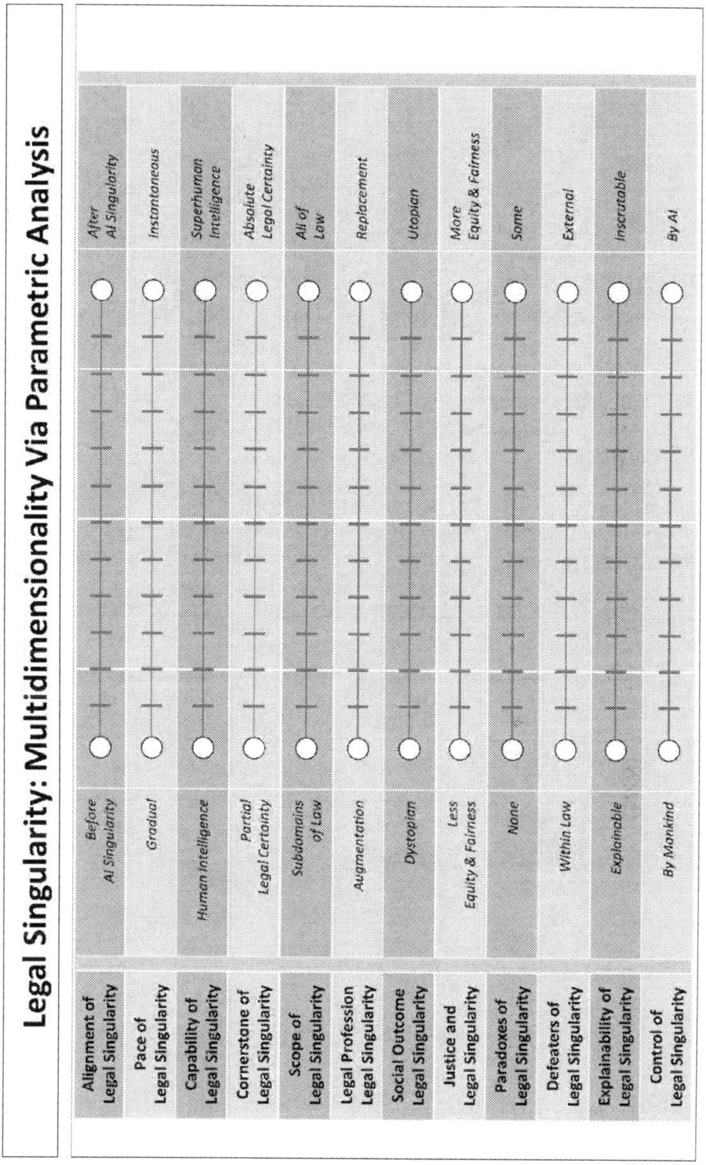

Figure 3: Legal Singularity Multidimensionality and Parametric Analysis

Source Author: Dr. Lance B. Eliot

Figure 6

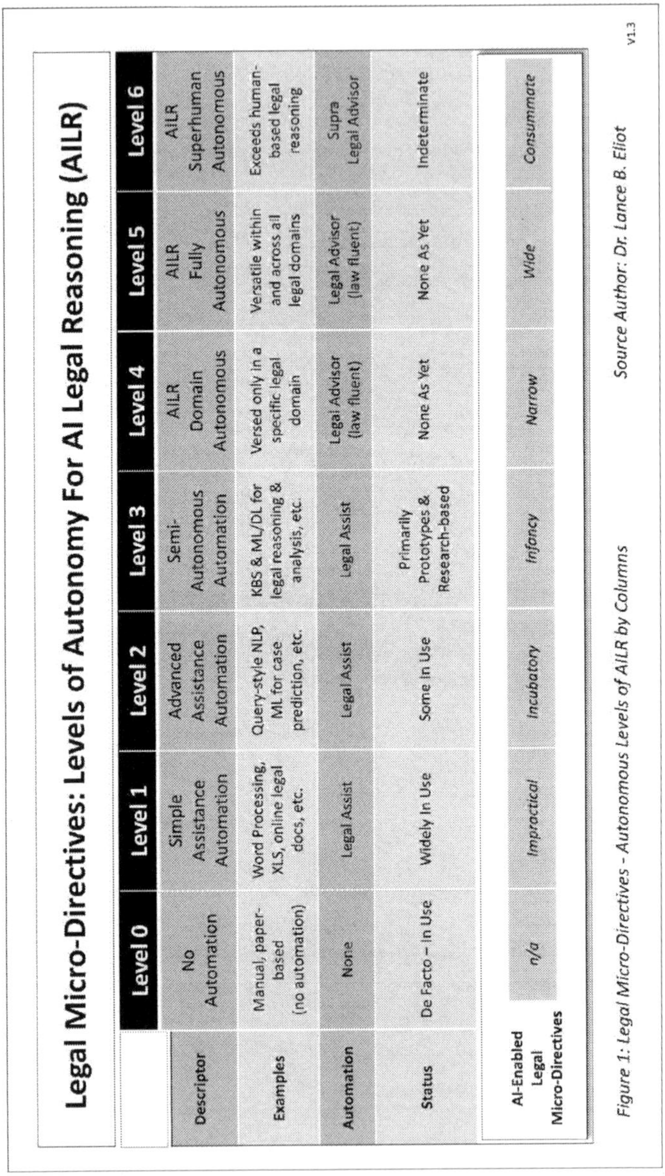

Legal Micro-Directives: Levels of Autonomy For AI Legal Reasoning (AILR)

	Level 0	Level 1	Level 2	Level 3	Level 4	Level 5	Level 6
Descriptor	No Automation	Simple Assistance Automation	Advanced Assistance Automation	Semi-Autonomous Automation	AILR Domain Autonomous	AILR Fully Autonomous	AILR Superhuman Autonomous
Examples	Manual, paper-based (no automation)	Word Processing, XLS, online legal docs, etc.	Query-style NLP, ML for case prediction, etc.	KBS & ML/DL for legal reasoning & analysis, etc.	Versed only in a specific legal domain	Versatile within and across all legal domains	Exceeds human-based legal reasoning
Automation	None	Legal Assist	Legal Assist	Legal Assist	Legal Advisor (law fluent)	Legal Advisor (law fluent)	Supra Legal Advisor
Status	De Facto – In Use	Widely In Use	Some In Use	Primarily Prototypes & Research-based	None As Yet	None As Yet	Indeterminate
AI-Enabled Legal Micro-Directives	*n/a*	*Impractical*	*Incubatory*	*Infancy*	*Narrow*	*Wide*	*Consummate*

Figure 1: Legal Micro-Directives - Autonomous Levels of AILR by Columns

Source Author: Dr. Lance B. Eliot

v1.3

Figure 7

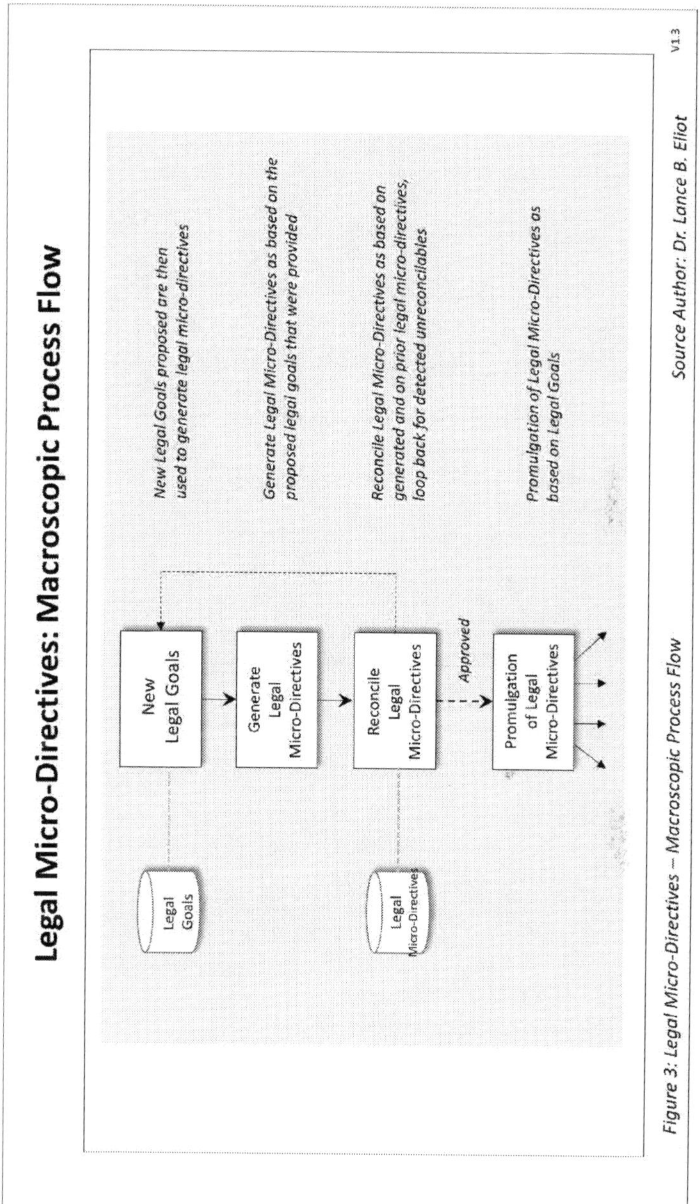
Legal Micro-Directives: Macroscopic Process Flow
Legal Goals
Legal Micro-Directives
New Legal Goals
Generate Legal Micro-Directives
Reconcile Legal Micro-Directives
Approved
Promulgation of Legal Micro-Directives
New Legal Goals proposed are then used to generate legal micro-directives
Generate Legal Micro-Directives as based on the proposed legal goals that were provided
Reconcile Legal Micro-Directives as based on generated and on prior legal micro-directives, loop back for detected unreconcilables
Promulgation of Legal Micro-Directives as based on Legal Goals
Figure 3: Legal Micro-Directives – Macroscopic Process Flow
Source Author: Dr. Lance B. Eliot
V1.3

Figure 8

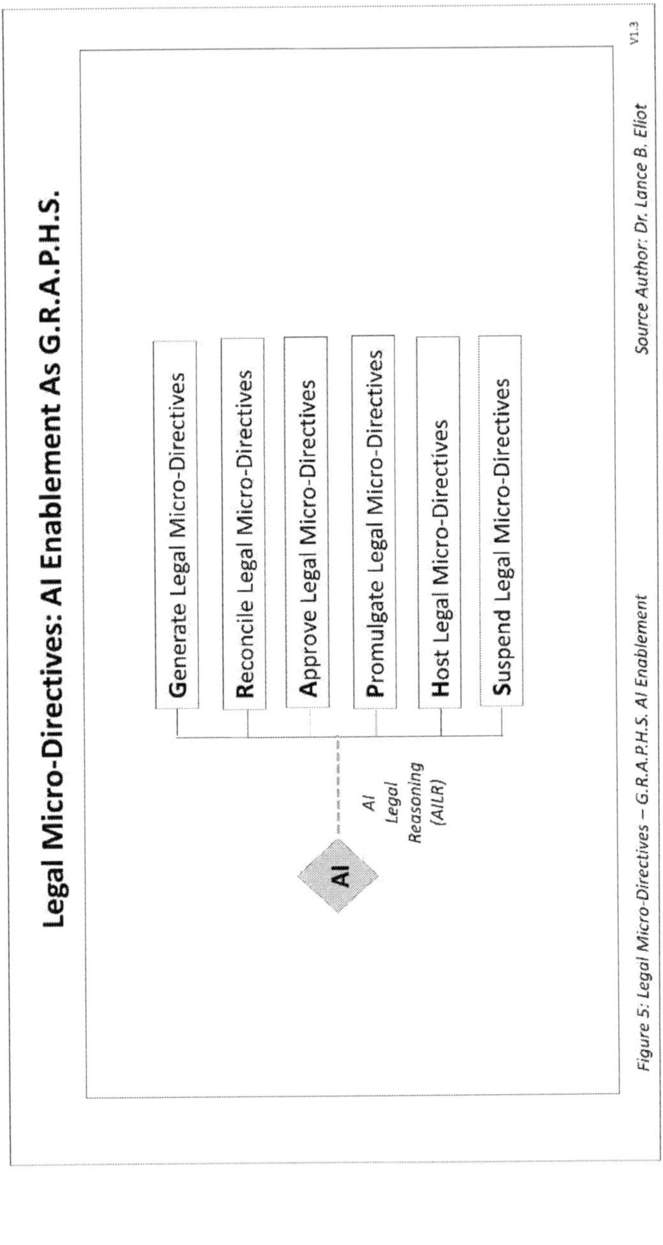
Legal Micro-Directives: AI Enablement As G.R.A.P.H.S.
AI
AI Legal Reasoning (AILR)
Generate Legal Micro-Directives
Reconcile Legal Micro-Directives
Approve Legal Micro-Directives
Promulgate Legal Micro-Directives
Host Legal Micro-Directives
Suspend Legal Micro-Directives
Figure 5: Legal Micro-Directives – G.R.A.P.H.S. AI Enablement
Source Author: Dr. Lance B. Eliot
V1.3

Figure 9

Legal Argumentation: Levels of Autonomy For AI Legal Reasoning (AILR)

	Level 0	Level 1	Level 2	Level 3	Level 4	Level 5	Level 6
Descriptor	No Automation	Simple Assistance Automation	Advanced Assistance Automation	Semi-Autonomous Automation	AILR Domain Autonomous	AILR Fully Autonomous	AILR Superhuman Autonomous
Examples	Manual, paper-based (no automation)	Word Processing, XLS, online legal docs, etc.	Query-style NLP, ML for case prediction, etc.	KBS & ML/DL for legal reasoning & analysis, etc.	Versed only in a specific legal domain	Versatile within and across all legal domains	Exceeds human-based legal reasoning
Automation	None	Legal Assist	Legal Assist	Legal Assist	Legal Advisor (law fluent)	Legal Advisor (law fluent)	Supra Legal Advisor
Status	De Facto -- In Use	Widely In Use	Some In Use	Primarily Prototypes & Research-based	None As Yet	None As Yet	Indeterminate
AI-Enabled Legal Argumentation	n/a	*Mechanistic (Low)*	*Mechanistic (High)*	*Expressive*	*Domain Fluency*	*Full Fluency*	*Meta-Fluency*

Figure 7: AI Legal Argumentation (AILA) - Autonomous Levels of AILR by Columns *Source Author: Dr. Lance B. Eliot*

V1.3

Figure 10

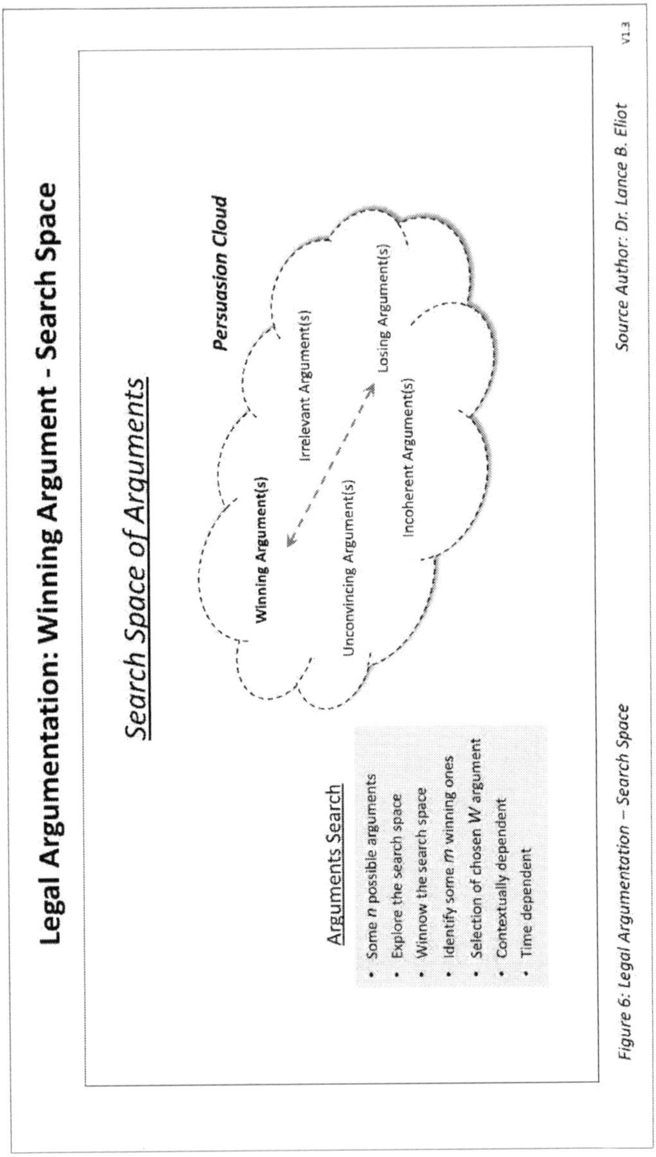
Legal Argumentation: Winning Argument - Search Space
Search Space of Arguments
Persuasion Cloud
Winning Argument(s)
Irrelevant Argument(s)
Losing Argument(s)
Unconvincing Argument(s)
Incoherent Argument(s)
Arguments Search
• Some n possible arguments
• Explore the search space
• Winnow the search space
• Identify some m winning ones
• Selection of chosen W argument
• Contextually dependent
• Time dependent
Figure 6: Legal Argumentation – Search Space
Source Author: Dr. Lance B. Eliot
V1.3

Figure 11

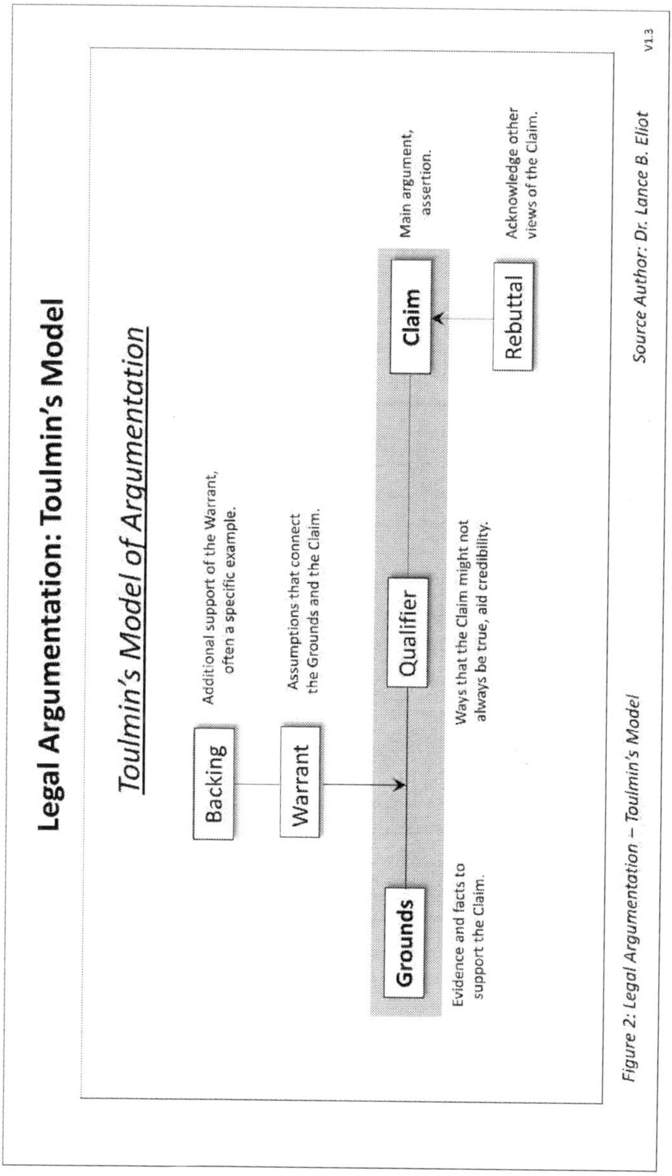
Legal Argumentation: Toulmin's Model
Toulmin's Model of Argumentation
Backing
Additional support of the Warrant, often a specific example.
Warrant
Assumptions that connect the Grounds and the Claim.
Grounds
Evidence and facts to support the Claim.
Qualifier
Ways that the Claim might not always be true, aid credibility.
Claim
Main argument, assertion.
Rebuttal
Acknowledge other views of the Claim.
Figure 2: Legal Argumentation – Toulmin's Model
Source Author: Dr. Lance B. Eliot
V1.3

Figure 12

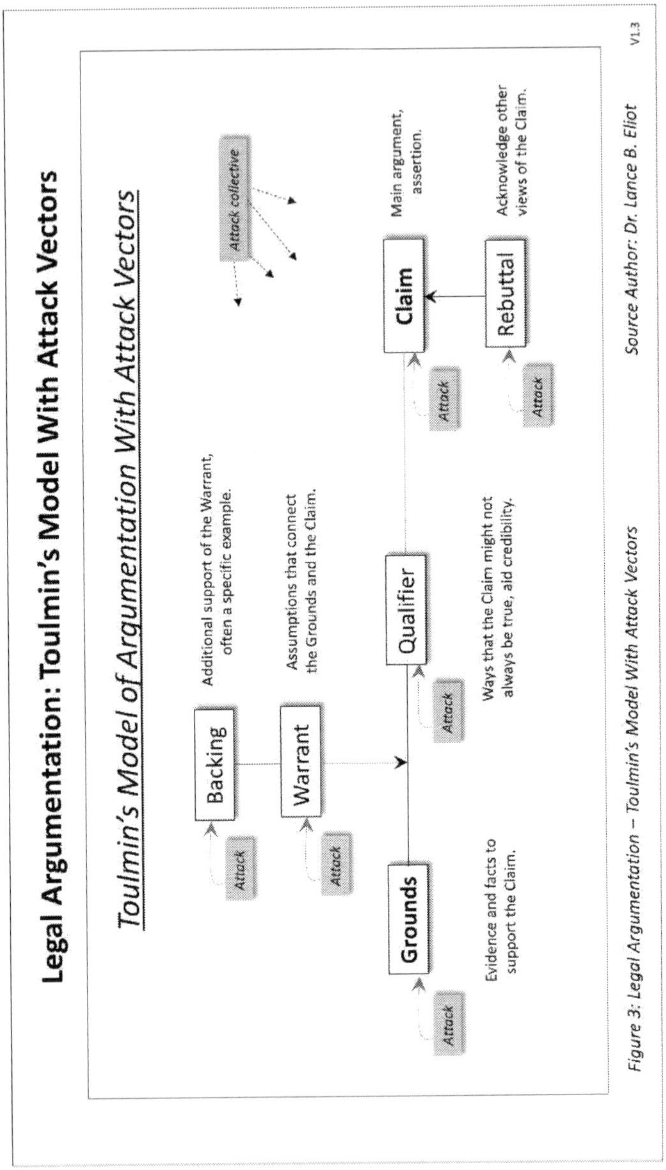
Legal Argumentation: Toulmin's Model With Attack Vectors
Toulmin's Model of Argumentation With Attack Vectors
Attack collective
Attack
Backing
Additional support of the Warrant, often a specific example.
Attack
Warrant
Assumptions that connect the Grounds and the Claim.
Attack
Grounds
Evidence and facts to support the Claim.
Attack
Qualifier
Ways that the Claim might not always be true, aid credibility.
Attack
Claim
Main argument, assertion.
Attack
Rebuttal
Acknowledge other views of the Claim.
Figure 3: Legal Argumentation – Toulmin's Model With Attack Vectors
Source Author: Dr. Lance B. Eliot
V1.3

Figure 13

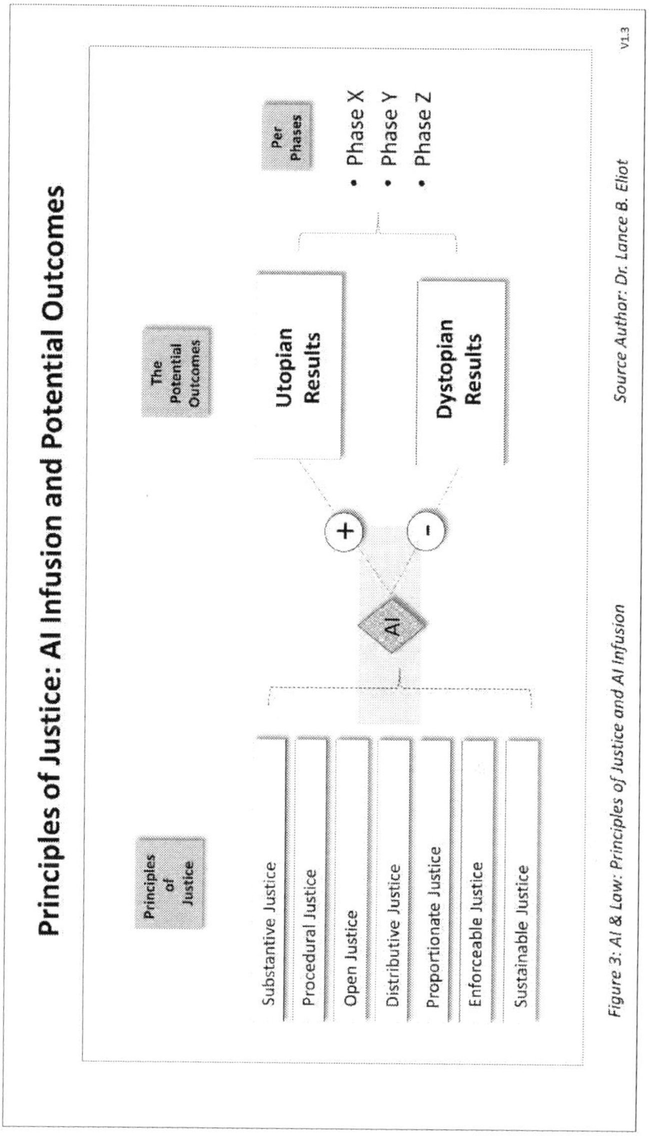

Figure 3: AI & Law: Principles of Justice and AI Infusion

Source Author: Dr. Lance B. Eliot

Figure 14

Principles of Justice and Autonomous Levels of AI Legal Reasoning (AILR)

	Level 0	Level 1	Level 2	Level 3	Level 4	Level 5	Level 6
Descriptor	No Automation	Simple Assistance Automation	Advanced Assistance Automation	Semi-Autonomous Automation	AILR Domain Autonomous	AILR Fully Autonomous	AILR Superhuman Autonomous
Substantive Justice	*Traditional*	*Traditional*	*Traditional*	Emerging	Phase X Impacts	Phase Y Impacts	Phase Z Impacts
Procedural Justice	*Traditional*	*Traditional*	*Traditional*	Emerging	Phase X Impacts	Phase Y Impacts	Phase Z Impacts
Open Justice	*Traditional*	*Traditional*	*Traditional*	Emerging	Phase X Impacts	Phase Y Impacts	Phase Z Impacts
Distributive Justice	*Traditional*	*Traditional*	*Traditional*	Emerging	Phase X Impacts	Phase Y Impacts	Phase Z Impacts
Proportionate Justice	*Traditional*	*Traditional*	*Traditional*	Emerging	Phase X Impacts	Phase Y Impacts	Phase Z Impacts
Enforceable Justice	*Traditional*	*Traditional*	*Traditional*	Emerging	Phase X Impacts	Phase Y Impacts	Phase Z Impacts
Sustainable Justice	*Traditional*	*Traditional*	*Traditional*	Emerging	Phase X Impacts	Phase Y Impacts	Phase Z Impacts

V1.3

Figure 1: AI & Law – Principles of Justice and LoA AILR by Columns

Source Author: Dr. Lance B. Eliot

Figure 15

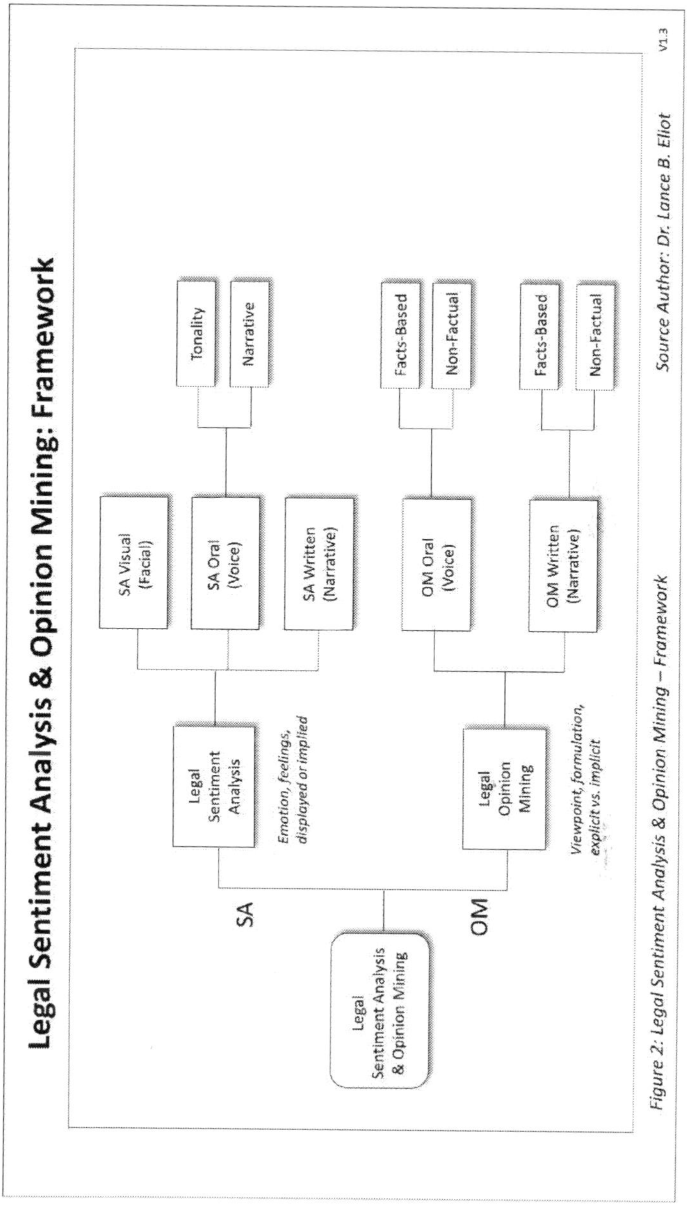
Legal Sentiment Analysis & Opinion Mining: Framework
Legal Sentiment Analysis & Opinion Mining
SA
OM
Legal Sentiment Analysis
Emotion, feelings, displayed or implied
Legal Opinion Mining
Viewpoint, formulation, explicit vs. implicit
SA Visual (Facial)
SA Oral (Voice)
SA Written (Narrative)
OM Oral (Voice)
OM Written (Narrative)
Tonality
Narrative
Facts-Based
Non-Factual
Facts-Based
Non-Factual
Figure 2: Legal Sentiment Analysis & Opinion Mining – Framework
Source Author: Dr. Lance B. Eliot
V1.3

Figure 16

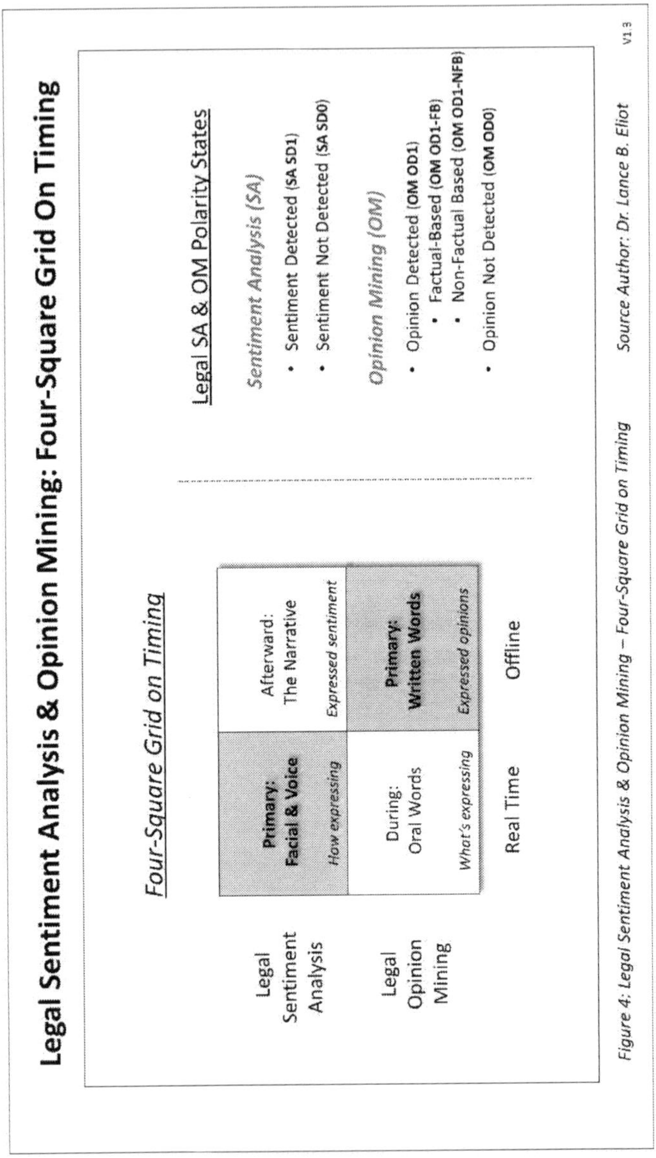
Legal Sentiment Analysis & Opinion Mining: Four-Square Grid On Timing
Four-Square Grid on Timing
Legal Sentiment Analysis
Legal Opinion Mining
Primary: Facial & Voice
How expressing
Afterward: The Narrative
Expressed sentiment
During: Oral Words
What's expressing
Primary: Written Words
Expressed opinions
Real Time
Offline
Legal SA & OM Polarity States
Sentiment Analysis (SA)
Sentiment Detected (SA SD1)
Sentiment Not Detected (SA SD0)
Opinion Mining (OM)
Opinion Detected (OM OD1)
Factual-Based (OM OD1-FB)
Non-Factual Based (OM OD1-NFB)
Opinion Not Detected (OM OD0)
Figure 4: Legal Sentiment Analysis & Opinion Mining – Four-Square Grid on Timing
Source Author: Dr. Lance B. Eliot
V1.3

Figure 17

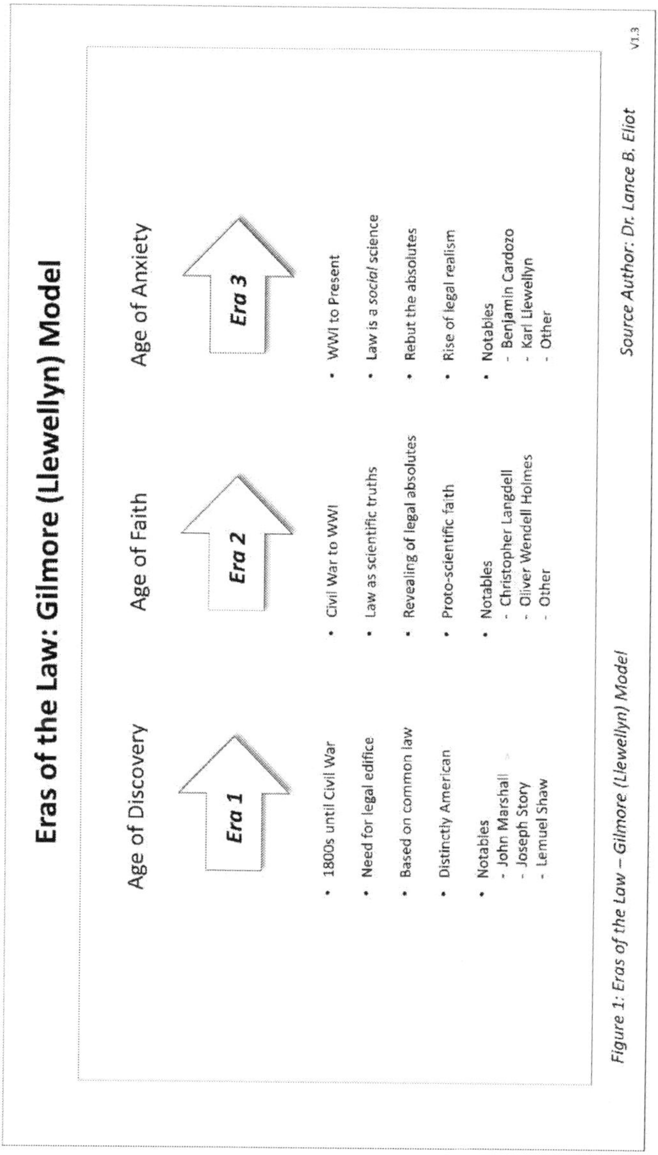
Eras of the Law: Gilmore (Llewellyn) Model
Age of Discovery
Era 1
1800s until Civil War
Need for legal edifice
Based on common law
Distinctly American
Notables
- John Marshall
- Joseph Story
- Lemuel Shaw
Age of Faith
Era 2
Civil War to WWI
Law as scientific truths
Revealing of legal absolutes
Proto-scientific faith
Notables
- Christopher Langdell
- Oliver Wendell Holmes
- Other
Age of Anxiety
Era 3
WWI to Present
Law is a social science
Rebut the absolutes
Rise of legal realism
Notables
- Benjamin Cardozo
- Karl Llewellyn
- Other
Figure 1: Eras of the Law – Gilmore (Llewellyn) Model
Source Author: Dr. Lance B. Eliot
V1.3

Figure 18

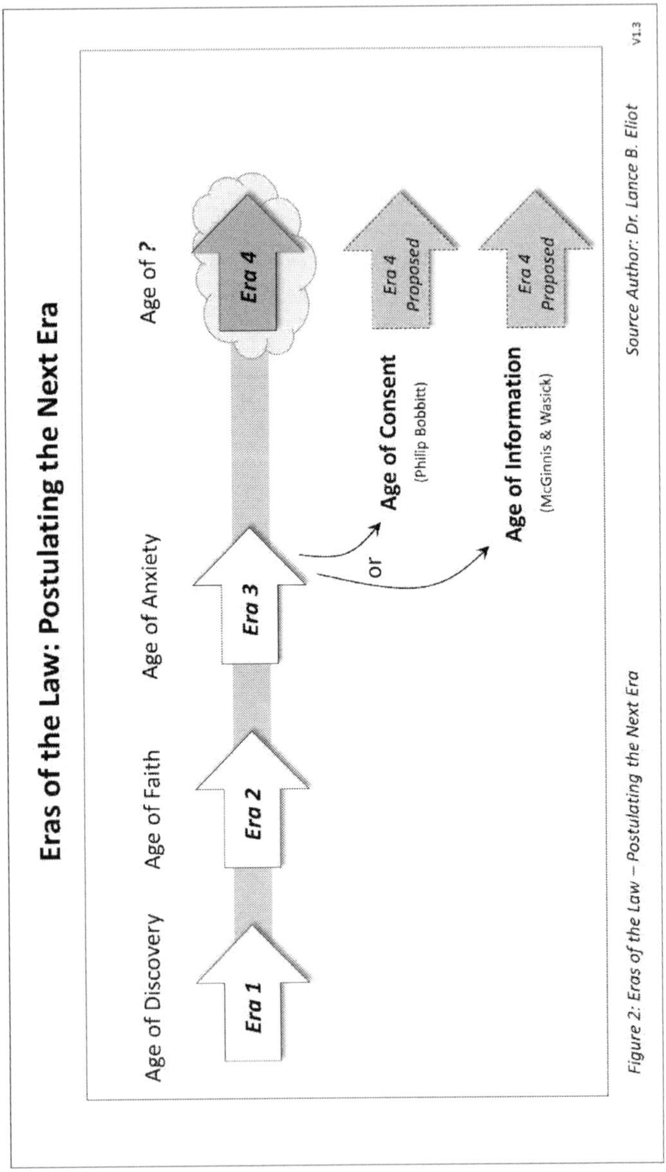
Eras of the Law: Postulating the Next Era
Age of Discovery
Age of Faith
Age of Anxiety
Age of ?
Era 1
Era 2
Era 3
Era 4
or
Age of Consent
(Philip Bobbitt)
Era 4 Proposed
Age of Information
(McGinnis & Wasick)
Era 4 Proposed
Figure 2: Eras of the Law – Postulating the Next Era
Source Author: Dr. Lance B. Eliot
V1.3

Figure 19

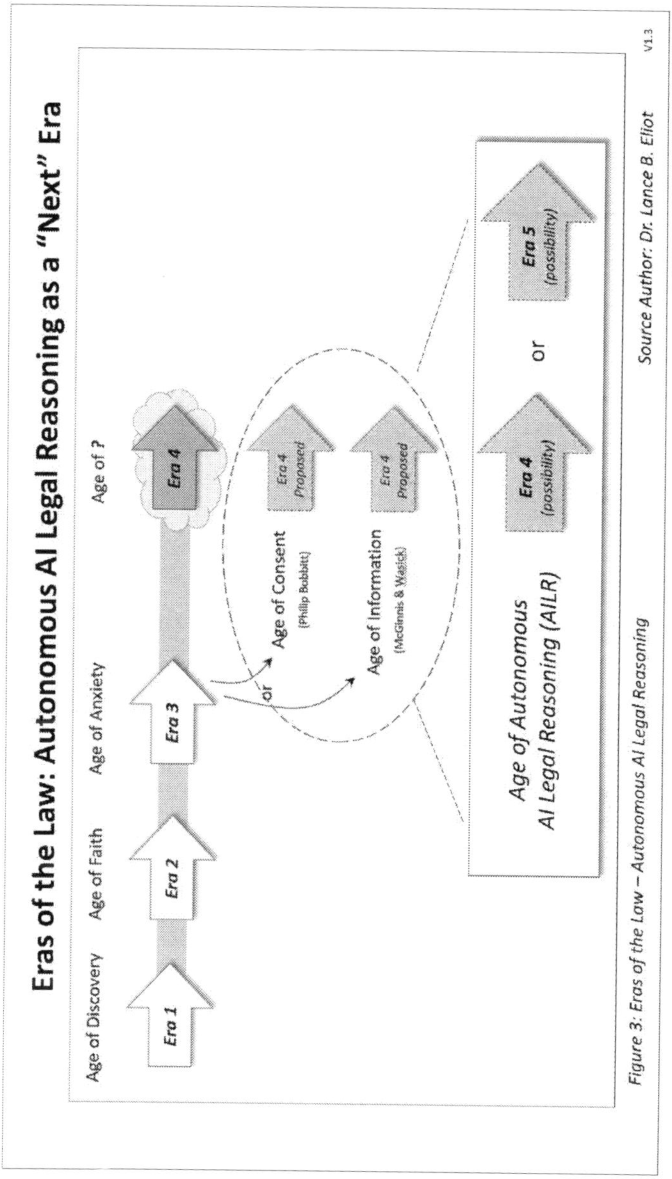
Eras of the Law: Autonomous AI Legal Reasoning as a "Next" Era
Age of Discovery
Age of Faith
Age of Anxiety
Age of ?
Era 1
Era 2
Era 3
Era 4
or
Age of Consent
(Philip Bobbitt)
Era 4 Proposed
Age of Information
(McGinnis & Wasick)
Era 4 Proposed
Age of Autonomous AI Legal Reasoning (AILR)
Era 4 (possibility)
or
Era 5 (possibility)
Figure 3: Eras of the Law – Autonomous AI Legal Reasoning
Source Author: Dr. Lance B. Eliot
V1.3

Figure 20

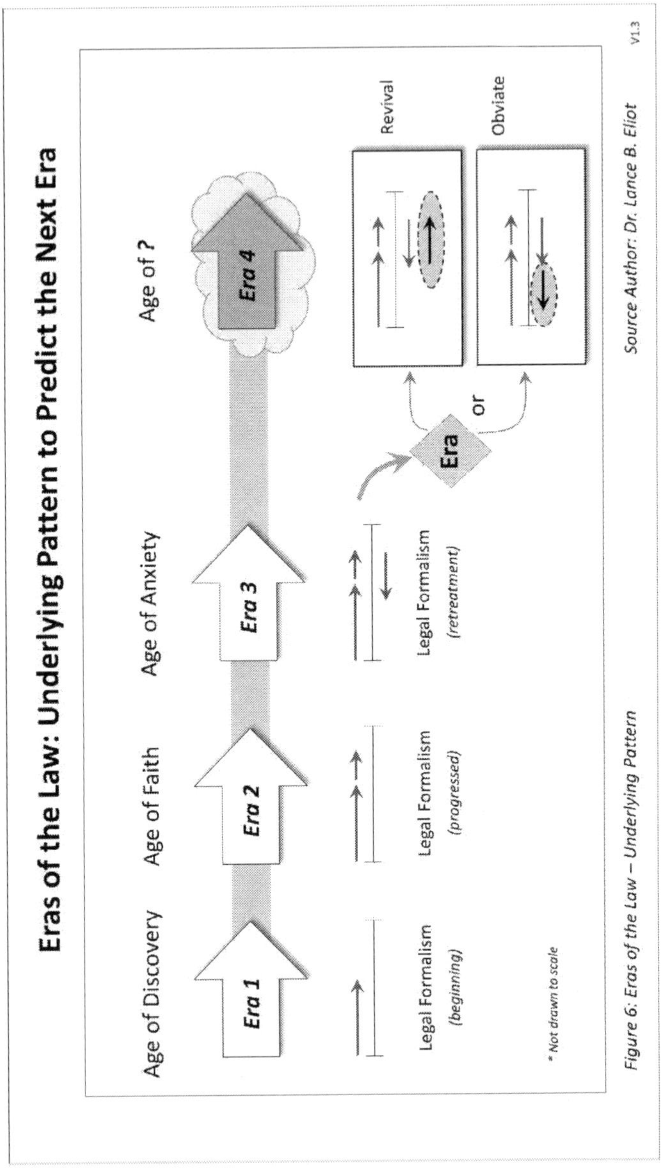
Eras of the Law: Underlying Pattern to Predict the Next Era
Age of Discovery
Age of Faith
Age of Anxiety
Age of ?
Era 1
Era 2
Era 3
Era 4
Legal Formalism
(beginning)
Legal Formalism
(progressed)
Legal Formalism
(retreatment)
Era
or
Revival
Obviate
* Not drawn to scale
Figure 6: Eras of the Law – Underlying Pattern
Source Author: Dr. Lance B. Eliot
V1.3

Figure 21

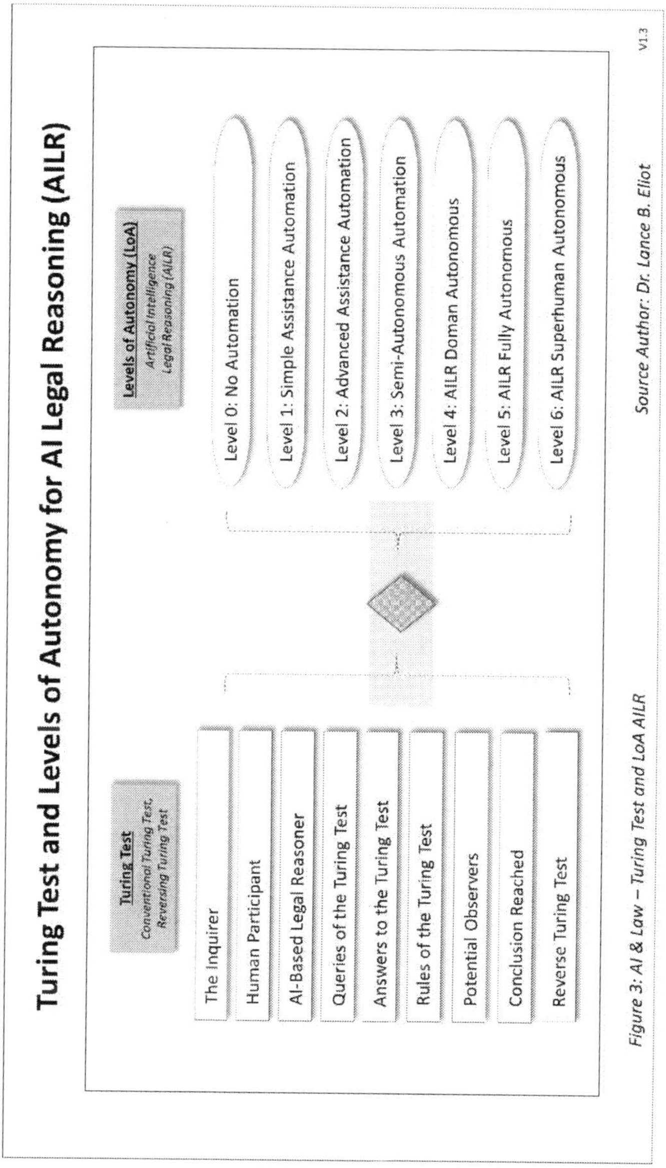
Turing Test and Levels of Autonomy for AI Legal Reasoning (AILR)
Turing Test
Conventional Turing Test,
Reversing Turing Test
The Inquirer
Human Participant
AI-Based Legal Reasoner
Queries of the Turing Test
Answers to the Turing Test
Rules of the Turing Test
Potential Observers
Conclusion Reached
Reverse Turing Test
Levels of Autonomy (LoA)
Artificial Intelligence
Legal Reasoning (AILR)
Level 0: No Automation
Level 1: Simple Assistance Automation
Level 2: Advanced Assistance Automation
Level 3: Semi-Autonomous Automation
Level 4: AILR Doman Autonomous
Level 5: AILR Fully Autonomous
Level 6: AILR Superhuman Autonomous
Figure 3: AI & Law – Turing Test and LoA AILR
Source Author: Dr. Lance B. Eliot
V1.3

Figure 22

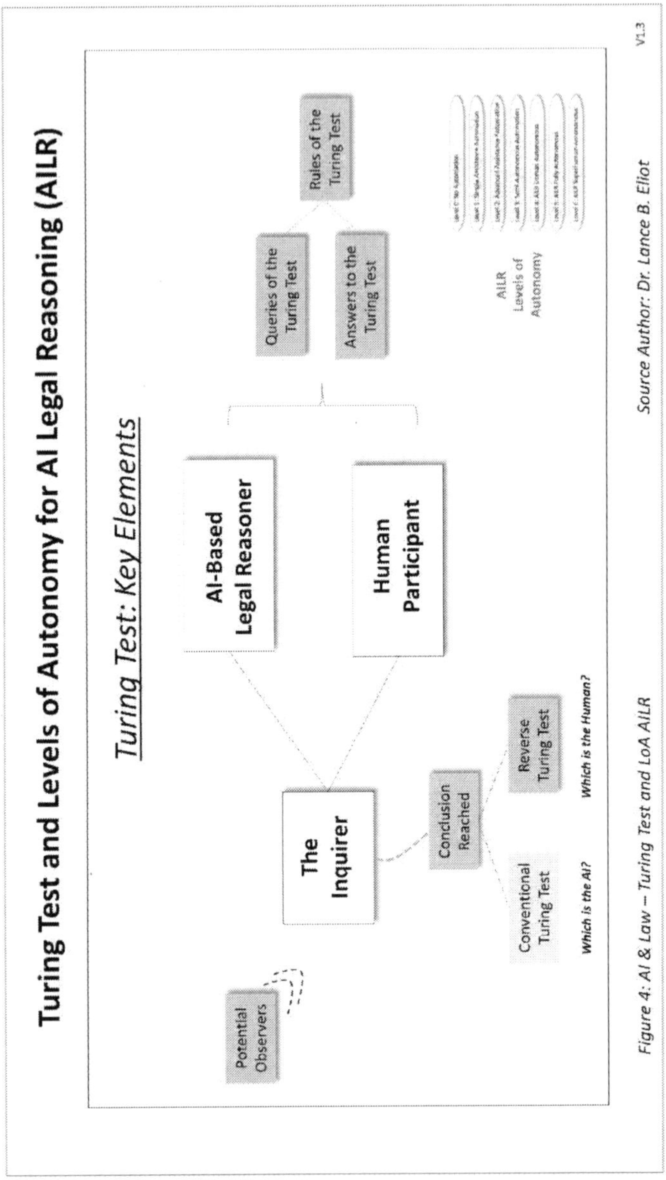
Turing Test and Levels of Autonomy for AI Legal Reasoning (AILR)
Turing Test: Key Elements
Potential Observers
The Inquirer
AI-Based Legal Reasoner
Human Participant
Queries of the Turing Test
Answers to the Turing Test
Rules of the Turing Test
Conclusion Reached
Conventional Turing Test
Reverse Turing Test
Which is the AI?
Which is the Human?
AILR Levels of Autonomy
Figure 4: AI & Law -- Turing Test and LoA AILR
Source Author: Dr. Lance B. Eliot
V1.3

Figure 23

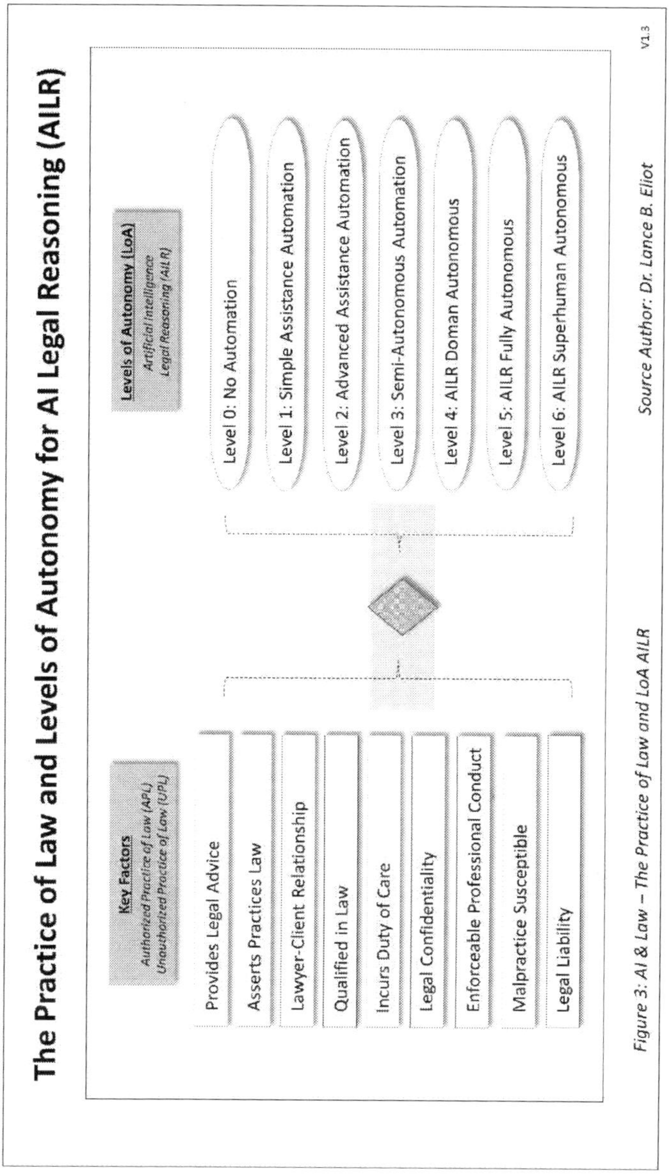
The Practice of Law and Levels of Autonomy for AI Legal Reasoning (AILR)
Key Factors
Authorized Practice of Law (APL)
Unauthorized Practice of Law (UPL)
Levels of Autonomy (LoA)
Artificial Intelligence
Legal Reasoning (AILR)
Provides Legal Advice
Asserts Practices Law
Lawyer-Client Relationship
Qualified in Law
Incurs Duty of Care
Legal Confidentiality
Enforceable Professional Conduct
Malpractice Susceptible
Legal Liability
Level 0: No Automation
Level 1: Simple Assistance Automation
Level 2: Advanced Assistance Automation
Level 3: Semi-Autonomous Automation
Level 4: AILR Doman Autonomous
Level 5: AILR Fully Autonomous
Level 6: AILR Superhuman Autonomous
V1.3
Figure 3: AI & Law – The Practice of Law and LoA AILR
Source Author: Dr. Lance B. Eliot

Figure 24

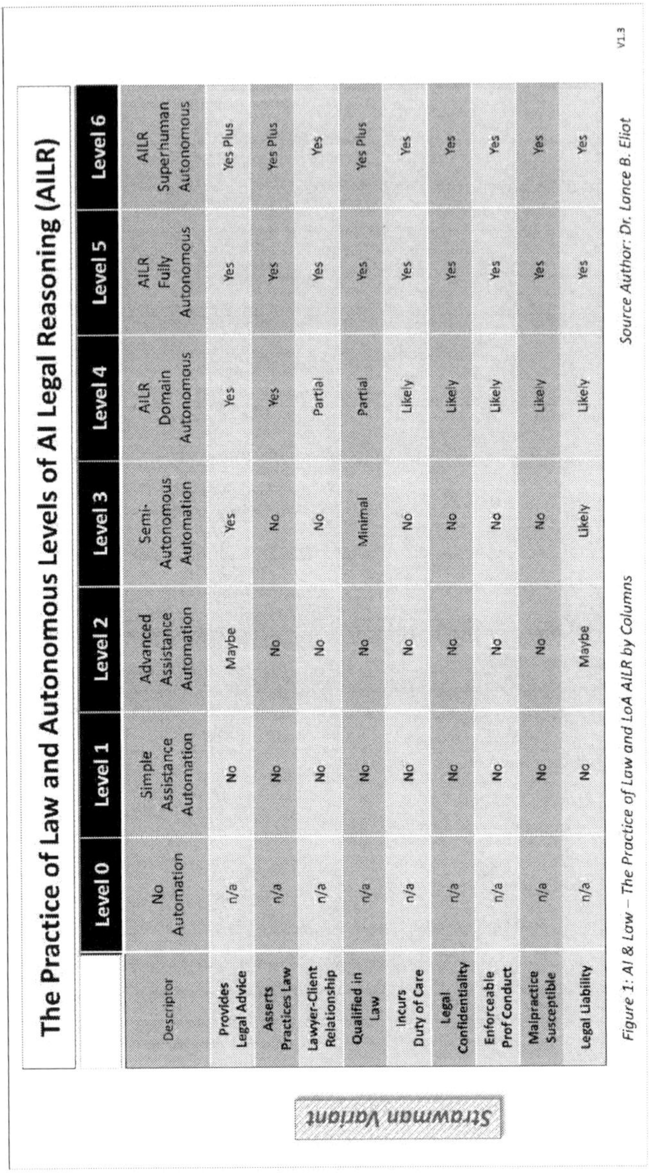
The Practice of Law and Autonomous Levels of AI Legal Reasoning (AILR)

Descriptor	Level 0 No Automation	Level 1 Simple Assistance Automation	Level 2 Advanced Assistance Automation	Level 3 Semi-Autonomous Automation	Level 4 AILR Domain Autonomous	Level 5 AILR Fully Autonomous	Level 6 AILR Superhuman Autonomous
Provides Legal Advice	n/a	No	Maybe	Yes	Yes	Yes	Yes Plus
Asserts Practices Law	n/a	No	No	No	Yes	Yes	Yes Plus
Lawyer-Client Relationship	n/a	No	No	No	Partial	Yes	Yes
Qualified in Law	n/a	No	No	Minimal	Partial	Yes	Yes Plus
Incurs Duty of Care	n/a	No	No	No	Likely	Yes	Yes
Legal Confidentiality	n/a	No	No	No	Likely	Yes	Yes
Enforceable Prof Conduct	n/a	No	No	No	Likely	Yes	Yes
Malpractice Susceptible	n/a	No	No	No	Likely	Yes	Yes
Legal Liability	n/a	No	Maybe	Likely	Likely	Yes	Yes

Figure 1: AI & Law – The Practice of Law and LoA AILR by Columns

Source Author: Dr. Lance B. Eliot

V1.3

Strawman Variant

Figure 25

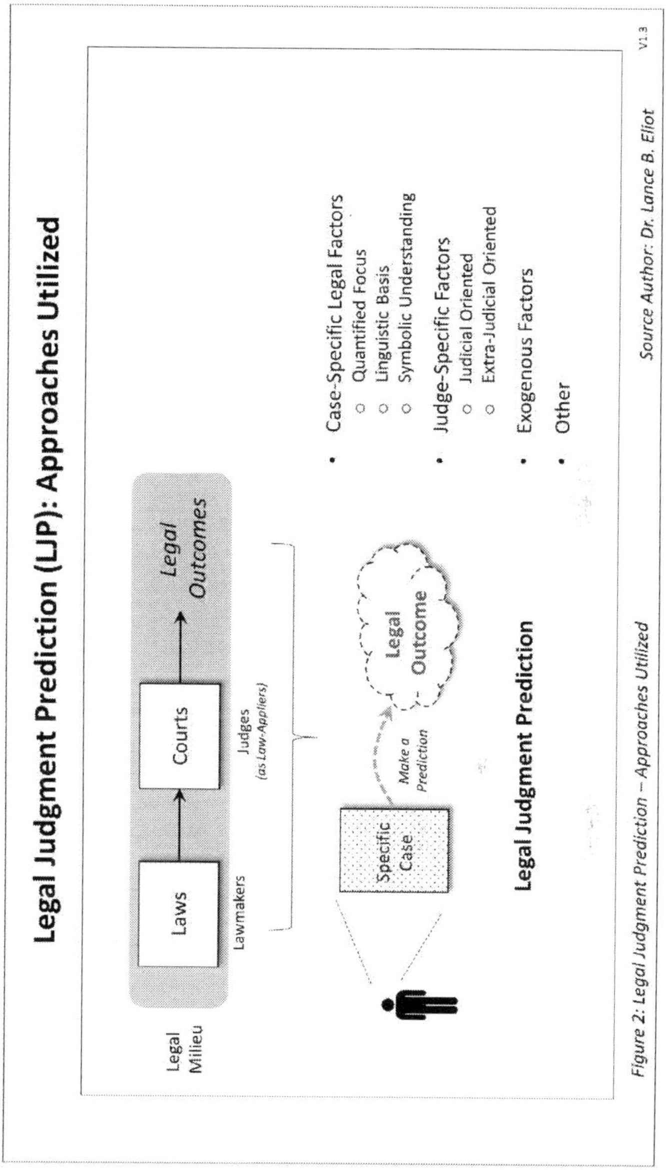
Legal Judgment Prediction (LJP): Approaches Utilized
Legal Milieu
Laws
Courts
Legal Outcomes
Lawmakers
Judges (as Law-Appliers)
Specific Case
Make a Prediction
Legal Outcome
Legal Judgment Prediction
Case-Specific Legal Factors
Quantified Focus
Linguistic Basis
Symbolic Understanding
Judge-Specific Factors
Judicial Oriented
Extra-Judicial Oriented
Exogenous Factors
Other
Figure 2: Legal Judgment Prediction -- Approaches Utilized
Source Author: Dr. Lance B. Eliot
V1.3

Figure 26

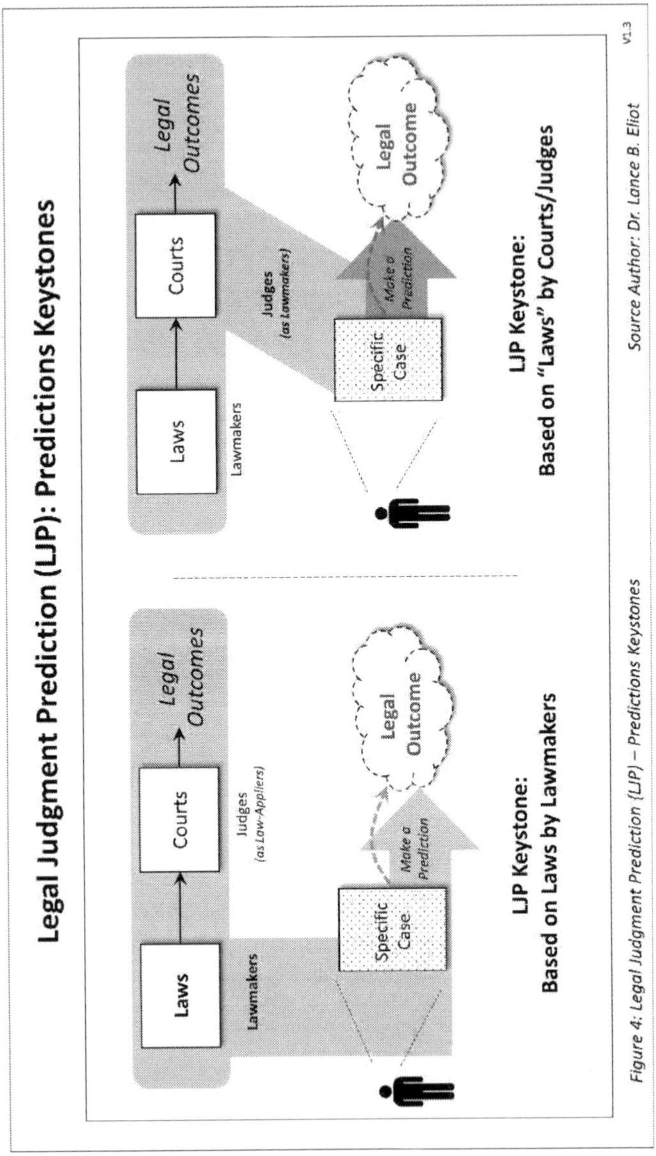
Legal Judgment Prediction (LJP): Predictions Keystones
Laws
Courts
Legal Outcomes
Lawmakers
Judges
(as Law-Appliers)
Specific Case
Make a Prediction
Legal Outcome
LJP Keystone:
Based on Laws by Lawmakers
Laws
Courts
Legal Outcomes
Lawmakers
Judges
(as Lawmakers)
Specific Case
Make a Prediction
Legal Outcome
LJP Keystone:
Based on “Laws” by Courts/Judges
Figure 4: Legal Judgment Prediction (LJP) – Predictions Keystones
Source Author: Dr. Lance B. Eliot
V1.3

Figure 27

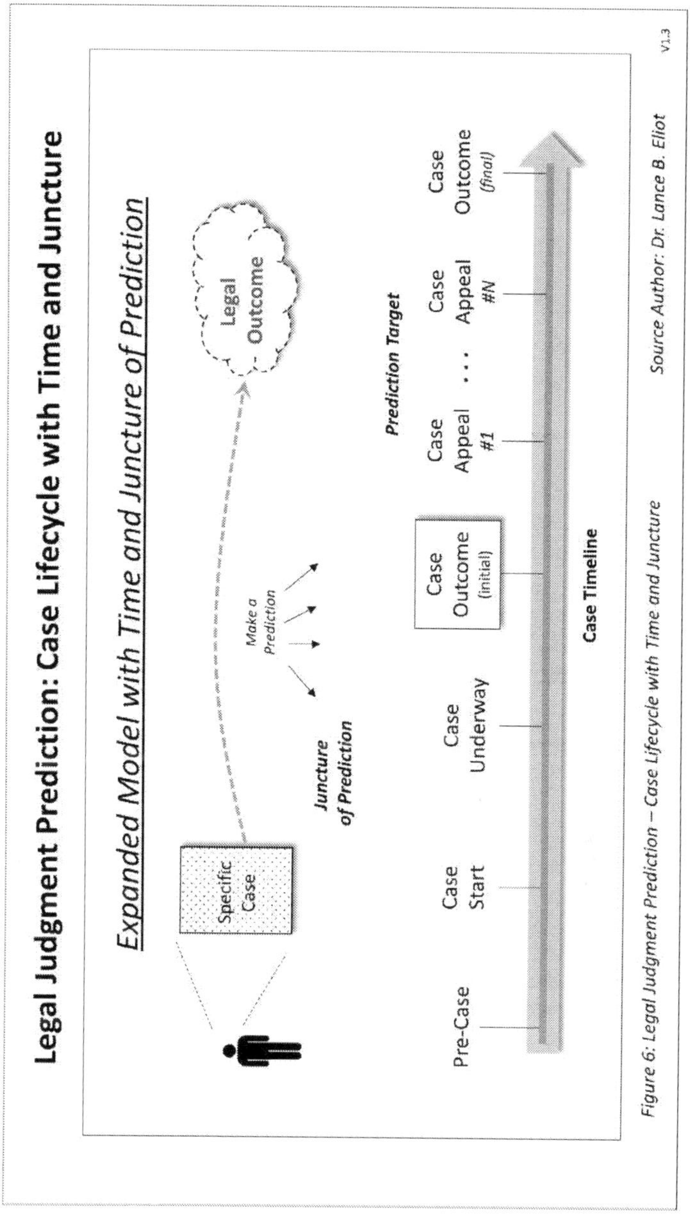
Legal Judgment Prediction: Case Lifecycle with Time and Juncture
Expanded Model with Time and Juncture of Prediction
Specific Case
Legal Outcome
Make a Prediction
Juncture of Prediction
Prediction Target
Pre-Case
Case Start
Case Underway
Case Outcome (initial)
Case Appeal #1
. . .
Case Appeal #N
Case Outcome (final)
Case Timeline
Figure 6: Legal Judgment Prediction – Case Lifecycle with Time and Juncture
Source Author: Dr. Lance B. Eliot
V1.3

Figure 28

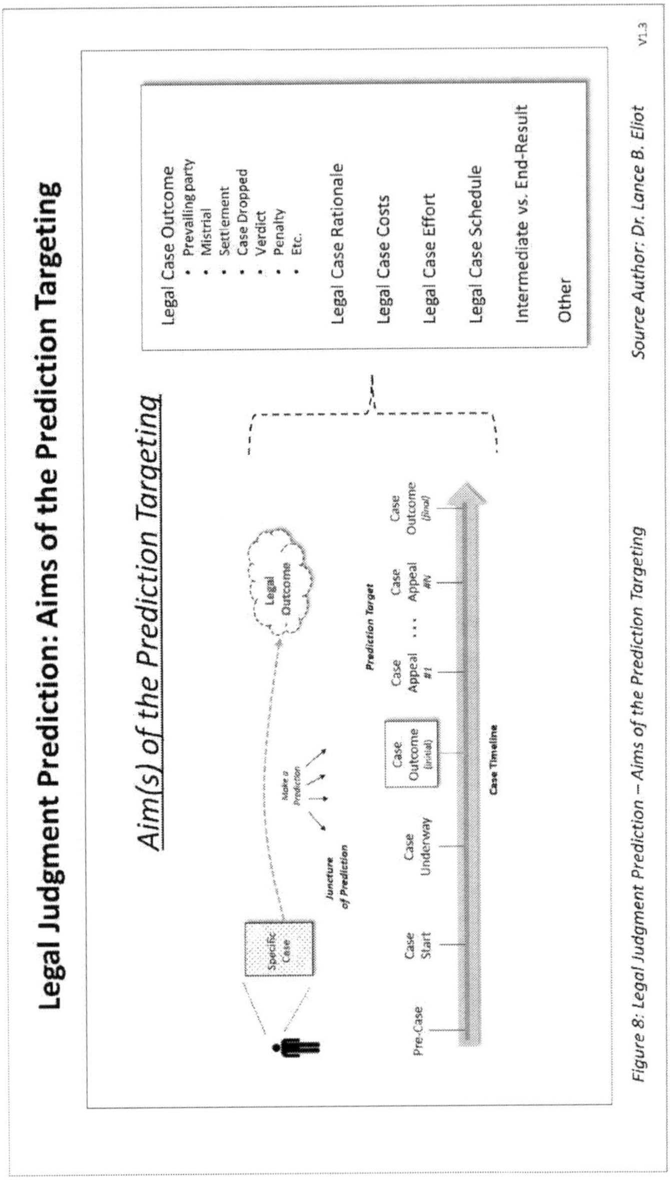
Legal Judgment Prediction: Aims of the Prediction Targeting
Aim(s) of the Prediction Targeting
Specific Case
Legal Outcome
Make a Prediction
Juncture of Prediction
Prediction Target
Pre-Case
Case Start
Case Underway
Case Outcome (initial)
Case Appeal #1
Case Appeal #N
Case Outcome (final)
Case Timeline
Legal Case Outcome
Prevailing party
Mistrial
Settlement
Case Dropped
Verdict
Penalty
Etc.
Legal Case Rationale
Legal Case Costs
Legal Case Effort
Legal Case Schedule
Intermediate vs. End-Result
Other
Figure 8: Legal Judgment Prediction – Aims of the Prediction Targeting
Source Author: Dr. Lance B. Eliot
V1.3

Figure 29

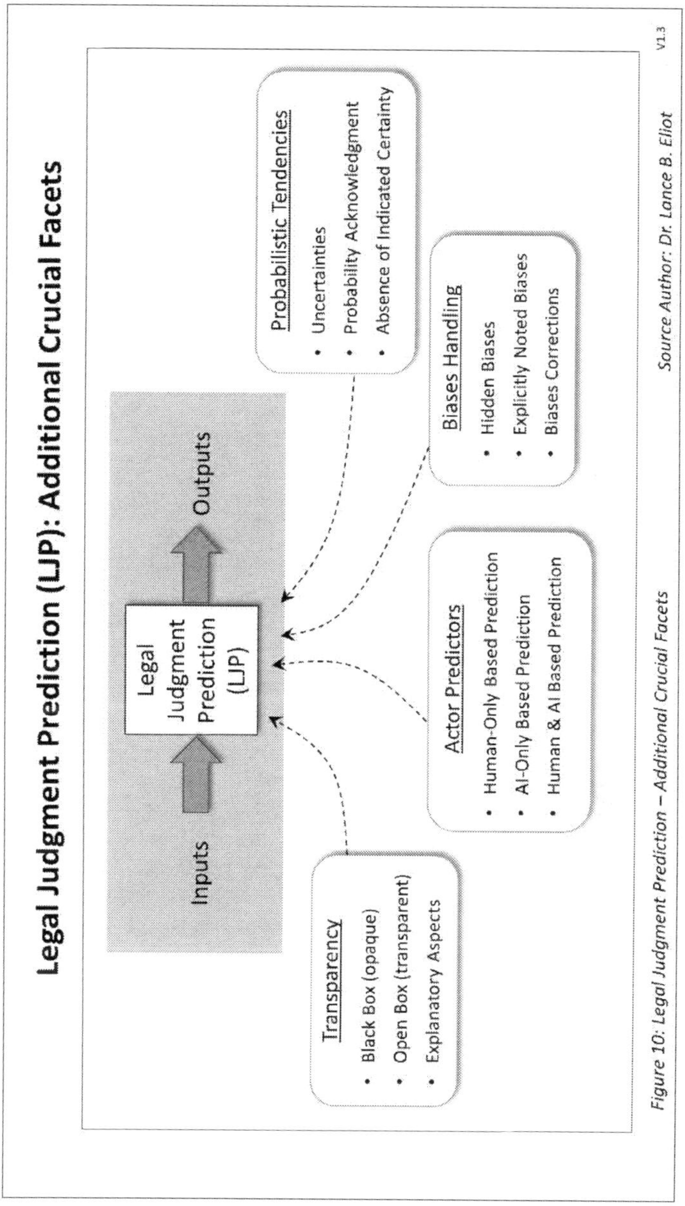
Legal Judgment Prediction (LJP): Additional Crucial Facets
Inputs
Legal Judgment Prediction (LJP)
Outputs
Transparency
• Black Box (opaque)
• Open Box (transparent)
• Explanatory Aspects
Actor Predictors
• Human-Only Based Prediction
• AI-Only Based Prediction
• Human & AI Based Prediction
Biases Handling
• Hidden Biases
• Explicitly Noted Biases
• Biases Corrections
Probabilistic Tendencies
• Uncertainties
• Probability Acknowledgment
• Absence of Indicated Certainty
Figure 10: Legal Judgment Prediction – Additional Crucial Facets
Source Author: Dr. Lance B. Eliot
V1.3

Figure 30

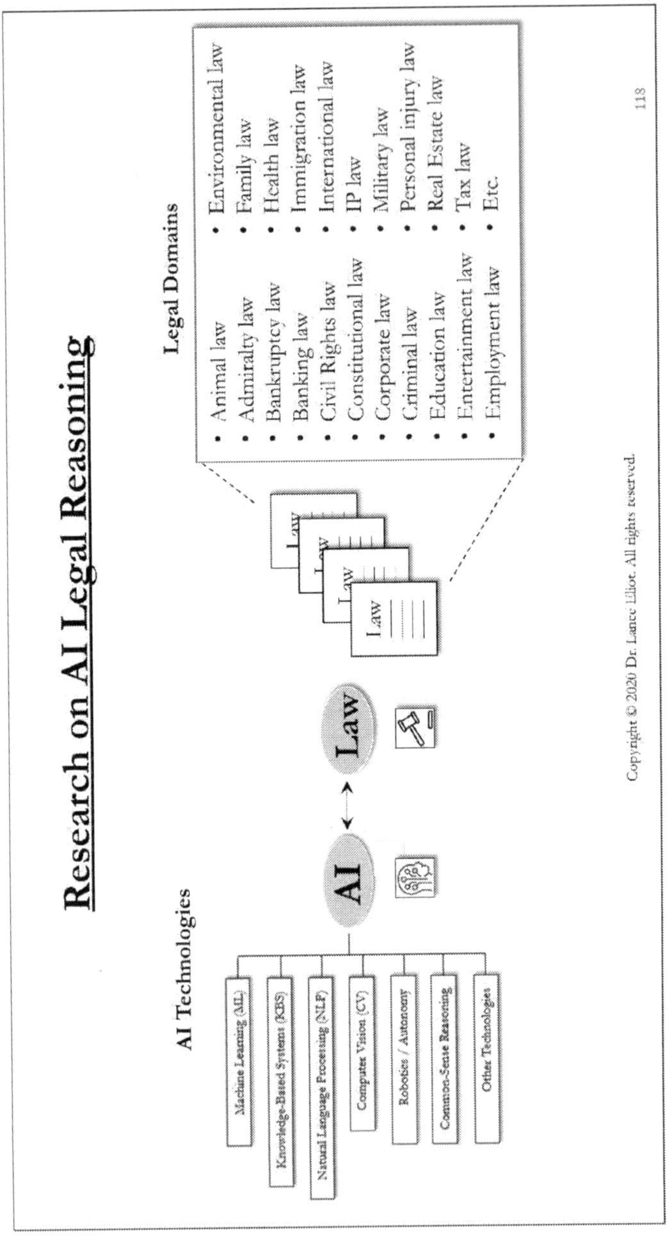
Research on AI Legal Reasoning
AI Technologies
Machine Learning (ML)
Knowledge-Based Systems (KBS)
Natural Language Processing (NLP)
Computer Vision (CV)
Robotics / Autonomy
Common-Sense Reasoning
Other Technologies
AI
Law
Law
Legal Domains
Animal law
Admiralty law
Bankruptcy law
Banking law
Civil Rights law
Constitutional law
Corporate law
Criminal law
Education law
Entertainment law
Employment law
Environmental law
Family law
Health law
Immigration law
International law
IP law
Military law
Personal injury law
Real Estate law
Tax law
Etc.
Copyright © 2020 Dr. Lance Eliot. All rights reserved.
113

Figure 31

ABOUT THE AUTHOR

Dr. Lance B. Eliot, Ph.D., MBA is a globally recognized AI expert and thought leader, an invited Stanford Fellow at Stanford University, an experienced top executive and corporate leader, a successful entrepreneur, and a noted scholar on AI, including that his Forbes and AI Trends columns have amassed over 4 million views, his books on AI are ranked in the Top 10 of all-time AI books, his journal articles are widely cited, and he has developed and implemented numerous AI systems.

He currently serves as the Chief AI Scientist at Techbruim, Inc. and has over twenty years of industry experience including serving as a corporate officer in billion-dollar sized firms and was a partner in a major consulting firm. He is also a successful entrepreneur having founded, ran, and sold several high-tech related businesses.

Dr. Eliot previously hosted the popular radio show *Technotrends* that was also available on American Airlines flights via their in-flight audio program, he has made appearances on CNN, has been a frequent speaker at industry conferences, and his podcasts have been downloaded over 150,000 times.

A former professor at the University of Southern California (USC), he founded and led an innovative research lab on Artificial Intelligence. He also previously served on the faculty of the University of California Los Angeles (UCLA) and was a visiting professor at other major universities. He was elected to the International Board of the Society for Information Management (SIM), a prestigious association of over 3,000 high-tech executives worldwide.

He has performed extensive community service, including serving as Senior Science Adviser to the Congressional Vice-Chair of the Congressional Committee on Science & Technology. He has served on the Board of the OC Science & Engineering Fair (OCSEF), where he is also has been a Grand Sweepstakes judge, and likewise served as a judge for the Intel International SEF (ISEF). He served as the Vice-Chair of the Association for Computing Machinery (ACM) Chapter, a prestigious association of computer scientists. Dr. Eliot has been a shark tank judge for the USC Mark Stevens Center for Innovation on start-up pitch competitions and served as a mentor for several incubators and accelerators in Silicon Valley and in Silicon Beach.

Dr. Eliot holds a Ph.D. from USC, MBA, and Bachelor's in Computer Science, and earned the CDP, CCP, CSP, CDE, and CISA certification.

Companion Book By Dr. Lance Eliot

"Artificial Intelligence and Legal Reasoning Essentials"

ISBN 978-1-73460165-7

Chapters

Available on Amazon and via other online book sellers

Companion Book By Dr. Lance Eliot

"Artificial Intelligence and LegalTech Essentials"

ISBN 978-1-7346016-3-3

Chapters

Available on Amazon and via other online book sellers

Companion Book By Dr. Lance Eliot

"Decisive Essays On AI And Law"

ISBN 978-1-73630310-8

Chapters

Available on Amazon and via other online book sellers

Companion Book By Dr. Lance Eliot

"Incisive Research On AI And Law"

ISBN 978-1-73630311-5

Chapters

Available on Amazon and via other online book sellers

Companion Book By Dr. Lance Eliot

"Ingenious Essays On AI And Law"

ISBN 978-1-73630312-2

Chapters

Available on Amazon and via other online book seller

Companion Book By Dr. Lance Eliot

"Compelling Essays On AI And Law"

ISBN 978-1-73630313-9

Chapters

<u>Companion Book By Dr. Lance Eliot</u>

"Topnotch Essays On AI And Law"

ISBN 978-1-73630314-6

Chapters

01 Introduction to AI and Law
02 AI & Law: Explainable AI (XAI)
03 AI & Law: Reversing False Memories
0 AI & Law: Antitrust and AI
05 AI & Law: Legal Aid Services
06 AI & Law: Bring Your Own Algorithm
07 AI & Law: Percolation of the Law
08 AI & Law: Rule of Law
09 AI & Law: British Nationality Act
10 AI & Law: Legal API
11 AI & Law: Ramification of Bad AI
12 AI & Law: Computable Contracts
13 AI & Law: C-Suite Buy-in
14 AI & Law: Standards for LegalTech
15 AI & Law: No Code
16 AI & Law: Human Signs of Dishonesty
17 AI & Law: Soft Law on AI
18 AI & Law: Regulating AI
19 AI & Law: Primer on AI and the Law
Appendix A: Teaching with this Material & Bibliography
Appendix B: Supplemental Figures and Charts
About the Author

Available on Amazon and via other online book sellers

Companion Book By Dr. Lance Eliot

"Trendsetting Essays On AI And Law"

ISBN 978-1-95-738601-0

Chapters

Available on Amazon and via other online book sellers

ADDENDUM

Thanks for reading this book and I hope you will continue your interest in the field of AI & Law

---

For my free podcasts about AI & Law:

https://ai-law.libsyn.com/website

Those podcasts are also available on Spotify, iTunes, etc.

For the latest on AI & Law see my website:

www.ai-law.legal

To follow me on Twitter:

https://twitter.com/LanceEliot

For my in-depth book on AI & Law:

AI And Legal Reasoning Essentials

www.amazon.com/gp/product/1734601655/